THE COMPLETE BOOK OF

CAKE
DECORATING

AUTHOR

Mary Ford

MARY FORD

Mary Ford is an acknowledged expert in the field of cake design and decoration, and in this book she shares her expertise in both traditional and innovative cake decorating skills. Mary has devoted her entire working life to creating exquisite cakes in her own unique style, and to passing on her craft to her students worldwide. Mary's established reputation as a leading author in the cake decorating field has led to a constant demand for a Mary Ford book to cover the many developments in cake decoration in the last ten years. This book has been written to satisfy that demand.

Mary's husband, Michael, works closely with Mary in planning and producing all her books. All the photographs are taken by him in their studio in England. He is also responsible for editing the books.

Mary Ford acknowledges with grateful thanks the assistance of Betty Nethercott and Mary Smith in creating items and cakes featured in this book.

Betty Nethercott was awarded a gold medal for cake decorating at Hotelympia, the international catering exhibition at Olympia in London. This prestigious award is one of the highest available in English sugarcraft. Betty is a judge for the British Sugarcraft Guild. Her interest in cake artistry began ten years ago when she attended an evening class. Through her natural talents in cake decorating, she quickly became a teacher for Hampshire County Council.

Mary Smith's interest in cake decorating was stimulated when she attended a six week royal icing course at the Mary Ford Cake Artistry Centre some nine years ago. Many of her talents are self-taught and her favourite medium for modelling is Mexican paste, creating items such as the Ugly Bug Ball. Mary ran her own cake decorating business before becoming head tutor at the Cake Artistry Centre in Bournemouth.

CONTENTS

© Copyright 1991 Mary Ford Publications Limited.
Published by Mary Ford Publications Limited,
294b Lymington Road, Highcliffe-on-Sea,
Christchurch,Dorset BH23 5ET, England.

Mary Ford stresses the importance of all aspects
of cake artistry, but gives special emphasis to the
basic ingredients and unreservedly recommends
the use of Tate & Lyle sugar.

Printed and bound in Hong Kong
ISBN 0 946429 36 7

Colour backdrops supplied by Robert Horne
Paper Company Limited, Eastleigh, Hampshire.

INTRODUCTION

"The Mary Ford Book of Cake Decorating" is my most comprehensive book to date and has been prepared as an invaluable reference book for the beginner and skilled cake decorator alike. This book is a follow-up to "101 Cake Designs" and "Another 101 Cake Designs" which have been international best sellers for the past decade. This new book has been written in response to the demand from colleges, cake artistry schools and cake decorators around the world for a Mary Ford book to cover the many developments and innovations in cake decoration in recent years.

A beautifully decorated cake forms the focal point for many of life's celebrations and this book offers designs that range from simple to stylish and elaborate. Beginners will find many designs which allow them to practise their developing skills, whilst experienced decorators will be challenged by the creative opportunties which unfold before them. As with all my books, the emphasis is on developing craftsmanship and practical skills. Over one thousand step-by-step photographs illustrate every stage of the decorating process and an introductory section covers the basics of equipment and preparation, with recipes and techniques clearly laid out for easy reference. Beginners should fully acquaint themselves with this section before beginning work.

Sixteen sections then cover in detail techniques such as sugarpaste modelling and bas-relief, floral artistry, piping tube embroidery, tulle work, painting with cocoa and piping gel, and the very new technique of rice paper artistry. Sections are included on royal icing designs, decorating sugarpaste coated and royal iced cakes, and a selection of wedding cakes to inspire the imagination. Each section includes a comprehensive introduction on how to use the technique and advice on achieving the best results. Celebration cakes for every occasion illustrate the technique and all the designs can be adapted to form the basis of an individual and unique cake which reflects your own personal skills and creative ability.

My aim is to introduce cake decorators to the basic technique, offer the opportunity to extend skills and develop confidence through practice, and then fire your own imagination. Beginners will find that, by practising the simple techniques such as buttercream, they will soon have the basis for a rewarding hobby. Enthusiasts, on the other hand, will find a wealth of information and advice on aspects such as design and colour choice as well as the more advanced and innovative techniques required for exciting cake decorating.

All the designs have been worked onto a prepared cake and it is a matter of personal choice whether the basic cake is a fruit or a sponge, or if it is coated in sugarpaste or royal icing. Irrespective of the finished design, the taste is still one of the most important aspects of a cake and the preliminary section of the book contains tried and tested recipes to ensure success.

Time and patience are the main ingredients for successful cake artistry and the steady hand which makes decorating easy comes from practice. Unless you are very experienced, it is always worth taking the time to practise the design first as this can avoid wasting the hours of preparation in the basic coated cake. An upturned cake tin, or any flat, wipe-clean surface, makes a useful 'dummy' on which to work and this is particularly useful when experimenting with incorporating aspects from different cakes into your finished design. As royal iced items are fragile, it is also worth making more pieces, such as collars or lace, than are required so that breakages do not hinder the work. Equally, timing is extremely important in planning a cake. Fruit cakes need time to mature and almond paste and coatings need time to dry before the work of decorating can commence. Many decorative items can be prepared in advance and stored until required. A rich cake should be completed at least two to three days before use, whereas a sponge should be made as late as possible to ensure freshness.

This book is both large and comprehensive, and inevitably some aspects of cake decorating belong in more than one section. Design, for instance, whilst fundamental to all cakes, is extensively covered in the wedding cake section at the end of the book. Royal icing, the use of which is found in almost every section, also has two specific sections devoted to it. However, by careful use of the detailed index/glossary, it is a simple matter to locate the appropriate recipe, technique, or advice that you require.

I hope that this book will stimulate your enthusiasm and help you in developing further your skills and expertise in the immensely rewarding, and increasingly popular, field of sugar artistry.

EQUIPMENT

Having the right equipment to hand makes cake decorating much easier, but it is possible to improvise if specialist equipment is not available. When purchasing equipment, always buy the best quality as this will not rust, bend or chip, and may last a lifetime with careful use. Always ensure that all equipment is scrupulously clean and free from grease.

Where possible, equipment such as wooden spoons and plastic bowls should be kept specially for icing as they can absorb strong flavours and taint icing during mixing or storage. Metal spoons and bowls, other than stainless steel, are not suitable as they may discolour the icing. Glass or earthenware bowls are ideal, provided they have no cracks which can harbour grease or dirt. A mixer is useful for making coverings and coatings.

If decorating cakes frequently, it is worth investing in a turntable as this makes the work much easier. A good turntable will be capable of supporting a heavy cake and will have a minimum diameter of 23cm (9") to enable safe carriage of a loaded 51cm (20") cake board. It must have a non-slip base and should be easy to turn when in use. However, a turntable for small cakes can be improvised by using an upturned cake tin or plate if necessary.

A good quality, smooth and heavy rolling pin about 45cm (18") will be needed for rolling out pastes, and nylon spacers can be helpful in achieving an even thickness. For modelling flowers, a smaller plastic rolling pin can be useful.

Stainless steel palette knives with firm blades are required for both mixing in colour and for coating cakes. An 18cm (7") and a 10cm (4") knife should be sufficient. A 38cm (15") straight edge is also required for smoothing royal icing or buttercream. This can be made of stainless steel or rigid plastic, and can be improvised with a stainless steel ruler if necessary. The sides of a cake can be smoothed using a palette knife, but purpose-made side scrapers make the task easier. Scrapers for cakes should be fairly rigid and are usually made of plastic.

Instructions for making a greaseproof paper piping bag are given in the preliminary section of this book, and this is recommended for all icing. Appropriate piping tubes are also illustrated and are readily available. Tubes should always be thoroughly washed immediately after use to remove the remaining icing before it hardens.

Much of the remaining equipment required, such as skewers, measuring jugs, nylon sieves, etc, will be found in most kitchens, and additional items such as a pair of compasses and fine paintbrushes may well also be available. However, all the tools and equipment required to complete the cakes in this book are obtainable from the Mary Ford Cake Artistry Centre, 28-30 Southbourne Grove, Bournemouth, Dorset, BH6 3RA, England, or local stockists.

SPONGE

This recipe produces a light sponge cake suitable for decorating and using immediately. It is particularly appropriate for coating in buttercream for children's birthday cakes but, if a novelty shape is to be cut out, then a genoese sponge (see p.12) is easier to shape and produces less crumbs.

RECIPE TABLES

TIN SHAPES			TIN SIZES		
ROUND	15cm(6")	18cm(7")	20.5cm(8")	23cm(9")	25.5cm(10")
SQUARE	12.5cm(5")	15cm(6")	18cm(7")	20.5cm(8")	23cm(9")
Fresh egg	60g(2oz)	70g(2½oz)	85g(3oz)	115g(4oz)	155g(5½oz)
Caster sugar	60g(2oz)	70g(2½oz)	85g(3oz)	115g(4oz)	155g(5½oz)
Self-raising sieved flour	60g(2oz)	70g(2½oz)	85g(3oz)	115g(4oz)	155g(5½oz)
Hot water	1 tsp	1¼ tsp	1½ tsp	2 tsp	2½ tsp
Baking temperature			204°C (400°F) or Gas Mark 6		
Baking test time	12 mins	13 mins	14 mins	15 mins	16 mins

BAKING TEST Bake the sponge for the required time, or until golden brown. Test for correct cooking by pressing the surface lightly with finger tips. If this leaves an indentation, continue baking. Repeat test every 2-3 minutes until the surface springs back when touched.

STORAGE The sponge may be wrapped in waxed paper and deep-frozen for up to 6 months. Use within 3 days of baking or after defrosting.

CHOCOLATE SPONGE Follow the basic sponge recipe but replace 15g(½oz) of flour with 15g(½oz) of cocoa powder for the 20.5cm (8") round sponge and pro rata for others.

HINTS AND TIPS

All equipment must be free from grease or the finished sponge will be heavy and lack volume.

Do not over-whisk the egg and sugar, as this will cause the batter to collapse.

Gently fold in the flour and do not over-mix or the sponge will not rise and the finished cake will be tough.

Do not allow mixture to settle on the side or edge of the mixing bowl, as otherwise 'streaking' will occur in the finished sponge.

Do not knock or drop the tin containing the mixture as air will be lost from the batter.

After pouring the batter into the tin, gently tilt the tin to spread the batter evenly over the base.

Bake immediately the batter is poured into the tin.

An oven which is too hot will produce a sponge of poor volume, flavour and shape with a highly coloured crust. This often produces a cake with an uncooked centre with numerous holes.

Too cool an oven will produce a pale, coarse sponge with a thick outer crust and very poor keeping qualities.

1

Preparing the tins: Grease the inside of the tin(s) with white fat, ensuring entire surface is covered.

2

Sprinkle sieved plain flour into the tin(s) and cover the greased surface. Tap out gently to remove excess flour.

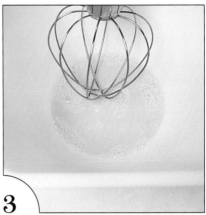

3

Making the sponge: Weigh all ingredients, using the appropriate quantity for the tin size (see p.10). Pour the eggs and sugar into a mixing bowl.

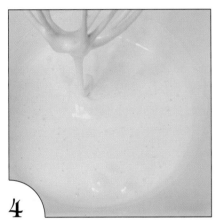

4

Whisk until the mixture is light and fluffy.

5

Stir in the hot water using a spoon.

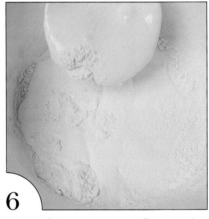

6

Gently fold in the sieved flour until mixture is smooth.

7

Immediately pour the mixture into the prepared tin(s).

8

Bake the sponges near the top of the pre-heated oven for recommended time. Then test as described on page 10.

9

When the sponges are baked, remove from oven and leave in the tin(s) for 5 minutes. Then turn out and leave to cool on a wire tray.

GENOESE

A genoese sponge has fat incorporated into the recipe, which produces a much closer and firmer texture than a light sponge and better keeping properties. As a genoese is easy to cut and shape, it is the most appropriate mixture for novelty cakes. It is particularly suitable for celebration cakes which require coating in sugar or almond paste, as it keeps well.

RECIPE TABLES

TIN SHAPES			TIN SIZES		
ROUND	15cm(6")	18cm(7")	20.5cm(8")	23cm(9")	25.5cm(10")
SQUARE	12.5cm(5")	15cm(6")	18cm(7")	20.5cm(8")	23cm(9")
Butter	30g(1oz)	45g(1½oz)	60g(2oz)	75g(2½oz)	85g(3oz)
Margarine	30g(1oz)	45g(1½oz)	60g(2oz)	75g(2½oz)	85g(3oz)
Caster sugar	60g(2oz)	85g(3oz)	115g(4oz)	145g(5oz)	170g(6oz)
Fresh egg (lightly beaten)	60g(2oz)	85g(3oz)	115g(4oz)	145g(5oz)	170g(6oz)
Self-raising flour (sieved)	60g(2oz)	85g(3oz)	115g(4oz)	145g(5oz)	170g(6oz)
Baking Temperature	190°C (375°F) or Gas Mark 5				
Baking test time	20 mins	22 mins	24 mins	26 mins	28 mins

BAKING TEST When the genoese has been baking for the recommended time, open oven door slowly and, if genoese is pale in colour, continue baking. When the genoese is golden brown, draw fingers across the top pressing lightly and, if this action leaves an indentation, continue baking. Repeat test, drawing fingers across top every 2-3 minutes until the top springs back when touched.

STORAGE When genoese is cold, wrap in waxed paper and store in deep-freeze for up to 6 months. Use within 3 days of baking or defrosting.

CHOCOLATE GENOESE Follow the genoese recipe but replace 30g(1oz) of flour with 30g(1oz) of cocoa powder for the 20.5cm (8") round sponge and pro rate for others.

HINTS AND TIPS

Ensure that all ingredients, including fats, are at 18-21°C (65/70°F) immediately prior to mixing.

Do not allow mixture to settle on the side or edge of the mixing bowl, otherwise 'streaking' will occur in the finished genoese.

The fat and sugar must be well beaten as otherwise the genoese will have poor texture and volume.

Add the egg slowly to the batter, as otherwise it will curdle and result in poor texture, volume, crumb structure and keeping quality.

To colour and flavour a genoese, carefully add a few drops of liquid food colouring and flavouring at the end of step 5.

It is important to gently fold-in the flour and not to over-mix as this will make a heavy mixture that will not rise and which will be tough with large holes in the finished cake.

After spooning the mixture into the baking tin, never knock or drop the tin as this will remove the air from the mixture.

1

Preparing the tins: Grease the inside of the tin(s) with white fat, ensuring entire surface is covered. Then place a disc of greaseproof paper in the tin(s).

2

Grease the greaseproof paper with white fat.

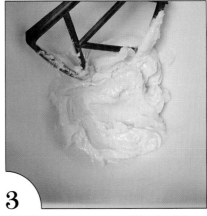

3

Making the genoese: Weigh all ingredients, using the appropriate quantity for the tin size (see p.12). Beat the margarine and butter until soft and light.

4

Beat in the caster sugar to form a light, fluffy consistency.

5

Thoroughly beat in the eggs using a small portion at a time.

6

Gently fold in the sieved flour, using a spatula. Do not overmix.

7

Spoon the mixture into the prepared tin(s) then smooth evenly with the spatula.

8

Bake in centre of pre-heated oven for recommended baking time. Then test as described on page 12.

9

When the genoese is baked, remove from oven and leave in the tin(s) for 5 minutes. Then turn out and leave to cool on a wire tray.

FRUIT CAKE

Fruit cake makes an ideal base for both sugarpaste and royal iced celebration cakes, and it is the traditional medium for wedding cakes as it has excellent keeping properties. Timing is important when making a fruit cake, as it needs at least three weeks to mature before use.

RECIPE TABLES

TIN SHAPES				TIN SIZES			
ROUND	15cm (6")	18cm (7")	20.5cm (8")	23cm (9")	25.5cm (10")	28cm (11")	30.5cm (12")
SQUARE	12.5cm (5")	15cm (6")	18cm (7")	20.5cm (8")	23cm (9")	25.5cm (10")	28cm (11")
Currants	170g (6oz)	255g (9oz)	340g (12oz)	425g (15oz)	515g (18oz)	600g (21oz)	680g (24oz)
Sultanas	170g (6oz)	255g (9oz)	340g (12oz)	425g (15oz)	515g (18oz)	600g (21oz)	680g (24oz)
Raisins	60g (2oz)	85g (3oz)	115g (4oz)	145g (5oz)	170g (6oz)	200g (7oz)	225g (8oz)
Candid peel (chopped mixed)	85g (3oz)	130g (4½oz)	170g (6oz)	215g (7½oz)	255g (9oz)	300g (10½oz)	340g (12oz)
Ground almonds	45g (1½oz)	65g (2¼oz)	85g (3oz)	105g (3oz)	130g (4½oz)	150g (5¼oz)	170g (6oz)
Grated lemon (rind & juice)	½	½	1	1	1¼	1½	2
Glacé cherries	60g (2oz)	85g (3oz)	115g (4oz)	145g (5oz)	170g (6oz)	200g (7oz)	225g (8oz)
Brandy	30g (1oz)	45g (1½oz)	75g (2½oz)	85g (3oz)	100g (3½oz)	115g (4oz)	130g (4½oz)
Plain flour (sieved)	115g (4oz)	170g (6oz)	225g (8oz)	285g (10oz)	340g (12oz)	400g (14oz)	455g (16oz)
Ground mace	small pinch	small pinch	medium pinch	medium pinch	large pinch	large pinch	large pinch
Ground spice (mixed)	¼ tsp	½ tsp	¾ tsp	1 tsp	1¼ tsp	1½ tsp	1¾ tsp
Ground nutmeg	pinch	pinch	¼ tsp	½ tsp	½ tsp	¾ tsp	1 tsp
Salt	small pinch	small pinch	medium pinch	medium pinch	large pinch	large pinch	large pinch
Butter	115g (4oz)	170g (6oz)	225g (8oz)	285g (10oz)	340g (12oz)	400g (14oz)	455g (16oz)
Sugar (soft brown)	115g (4oz)	170g (6oz)	225g (8oz)	285g (10oz)	340g (12oz)	400g (14oz)	455g (16oz)
Fresh egg (lightly beaten)	170g (6oz)	255g (9oz)	340g (12oz)	425g (15oz)	515g (18oz)	600g (21oz)	680g (24oz)
Baking temperature			140°C (275°F) or Gas Mark 1				
Baking time (approximately)	2¼ hrs	3 hrs	3½ hrs	3¾ hrs	4¼ hrs	5½ hrs	6½ hrs

BAKING TEST At the end of the recommended baking time, bring the cake forward from the oven so that it can be tested. Then insert a stainless steel skewer into the centre of the cake and slowly withdraw it. The skewer should be as clean as it went in. This means the cake is sufficiently baked. If cake mixture clings to the skewer, remove the skewer completely and continue baking at the same temperature. Test thereafter every 10 minutes until the skewer is clean when withdrawn from the cake.

STORAGE When the cake is cold carefully remove from the tin, then remove the greaseproof paper. Wrap the cake in waxed paper and leave in a cupboard for three weeks to mature.

HINTS AND TIPS It is important to line the inside of the cake tin carefully to prevent a mis-shape.

Add the egg slowly to the batter, as otherwise it will curdle and result in poor texture, volume, crumb structure and keeping quality.

If the batter starts to curdle, beat in a little of the flour. Thoroughly stir the flour into the batter before adding the fruit, but do not overmix as this will toughen the batter.

Flour is best added with a wooden spoon.

Overbeaten batter will not support the fruit, which will sink during baking. Make sure all cleaned fruit is as dry as possible. Do not overwash the fruit.

The cake mixture can be left to stand for up to 24 hours in the tin before baking if necessary.

Never bake a cake in a brand new, shiny tin. (The shine can be removed by placing the empty tin in a hot oven).

Too hot an oven will produce a cake which has a cracked, crusted top and an uncooked centre. It will be very dark in colour and have bitter tasting, burnt fruit around its crust.

An oven which is too cool will produce a pale cake with uncooked fruit and a very thick crust. The cake will go dry and will not keep.

If the cake has been baked at the correct temperature but sinks in the middle the cause may be too much liquid, sugar, fat or baking powder in the mixture.

If the cake is found to be crumbly, the following reasons could apply: curdled batter; overbeating the fat, sugar and eggs; undermixing the flour and fruit into the batter; insufficient sugar.

1 **Weighing**: Carefully weigh ingredients using appropriate quantities for tin size (see p.14). Leave ingredients in a warm place 18°C(65°F) for 12 hours.

2 **Preparing the tins:** Grease the inside of the tin(s) with white fat. Line with greaseproof paper and grease with white fat.

3 **Making the cake:** Beat the butter until light, then beat in the sugar until light and fluffy.

4 Thoroughly beat in the egg a little at a time until all the egg is used.

5 Carefully fold in the dry ingredients using a spatula. Do not overmix.

6 Add the fruit and pour in the liquids.

7 Stir thoroughly until all the fruit is well mixed.

8 Place the mixture into the tin(s) and spread evenly with a spatula.

9 Bake in centre of pre-heated oven for recommended baking time, then test (see p.14). Remove from oven and leave to cool for 24 hours.

BUTTERCREAM

INGREDIENTS

Butter   115g (4oz)
Icing sugar   170-225g (6-8oz)
Warm water   1-2 tbls
Food colouring or flavouring

Buttercream is an ideal medium for coating children's cakes as it is easily coloured and flavoured. To vary the taste and texture of buttercream beat in any of the following: whisked egg white, milk, egg, marshmallow, fondant, condensed milk, and edible colours and flavours. To obtain the best results, always use fresh butter at a temperature of 18-21°C (65-70°F).

1

2

3

Soften the butter and beat until it is light.

Sieve the icing sugar and gradually add it to the butter, beating well after each addition.

Add the warm water, and flavouring and colouring if required. Beat the mixture once again.

ALMOND PASTE

INGREDIENTS

Caster sugar   170g (6oz)
Icing sugar   170g (6oz)
Ground almonds   340g (12oz)
Glucose syrup   225g (8oz)

Almond paste differs from marzipan in that almond paste is a mixture of uncooked ground almonds, sugar and glucose, whereas marzipan is made from cooked ground almonds and sugar. Either paste is suitable for covering cakes. Almond paste can be stored in waxed paper or in a sealed container in a cool, dry place. Do not overmix the paste and never allow almond paste to come into contact with flour.
See pages 24, 25 and 168 for the method and advice on covering cakes.

1

2

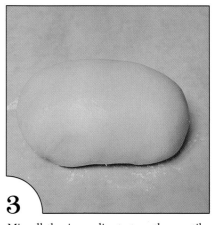

3

Sieve the icing sugar, then mix all the dry ingredients together.

Warm the glucose syrup and pour it into the dry ingredients.

Mix all the ingredients together until a pliable paste is formed. Store in a sealed container until required.

MEXICAN MODELLING PASTE

INGREDIENTS

Icing sugar	255g (9oz)
Gum tragacanth	1 level tbls
Liquid glucose	1 level tsp
Cold water	8 tsps

Mexican modelling paste is ideal for making the bodies of moulded figures, as seen on p.55. It can also be used successfully for making flowers.

Storage: Place in a food-approved polythene bag and store in an airtight container in a refrigerator. Bring to room temperature before use.

1 Sieve the icing sugar and gum tragacanth together into a bowl.

2 Combine the glucose and water and pour into the dry ingredients. Mix well.

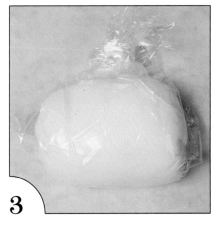

3 Wrap the modelling paste in a food-approved polythene bag and store in an airtight container.

PASTILLAGE

INGREDIENTS

Water	60g (2oz)
Gelatine	10g (⅓oz)
Icing sugar	500g (17½oz)
Cornflour	30g (1oz)
Royal icing	30g (1oz)

Pastillage is a paste used where strength is required, such as in the construction of the roof of the circus tent on p.47 and in pillars and top ornaments.

Storage: Place in a food- approved polythene bag and store in an airtight container in a refrigerator. Bring to room temperature before use.

1 Pour the water into a bowl. Sprinkle the gelatine over the surface and dissolve by standing the bowl over a pan of hot, but not boiling, water.

2 Sieve the icing sugar and cornflour into a second bowl and make a well in the centre. Pour in the dissolved gelatine and stir with a warm knife.

3 Stir in the royal icing then knead until smooth. Wrap the pastillage in a food-approved polythene bag and store in airtight container.

ALBUMEN SOLUTION

INGREDIENTS

Pure albumen powder	15g (½oz)
Water	85g (3oz)

When making albumen solution it is essential that all utensils are sterilised and free from grease.

When the albumen powder is mixed into the water, it will go lumpy. After 1 hour, stirring occasionally, the lumps will dissolve to form a smooth liquid. Once the solution has been made, it should be kept in a refrigerator in a sealed container.

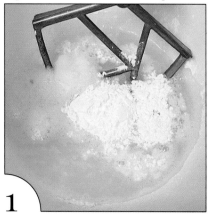

1

Pour the water into a bowl and stir whilst sprinkling in the powdered albumen.

2

Thoroughly mix with the whisk, but do not beat. Leave for 1 hour, stirring occasionally.

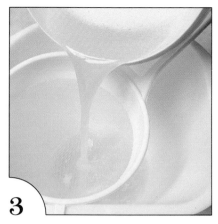

3

Strain the solution through a fine sieve or muslin. It is then ready for use.

ROYAL ICING

INGREDIENTS

Fresh egg white or albumen solution	100g (3½oz)
Icing sugar (sieved)	455g (16oz)

Note: If using fresh egg whites separate 24 hours before required.

GLYCERIN - Table for use

For soft cutting royal icing add to every 455g (16oz) of ready-made royal icing:-
1 teaspoon of glycerin for the bottom tier of a three-tier cake.
2 teaspoons of glycerin for middle tier of a three-tier cake.
3 teaspoons of glycerin for top tier or for single-tier cakes.

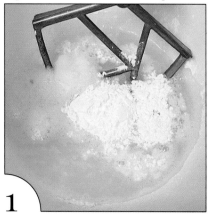

1

Pour the fresh egg whites or albumen solution into a mixing bowl. Stir in half the sieved icing sugar until dissolved.

2

Stir in remaining sugar and then clean down the inside of the bowl.

3

Beat mixture until light and fluffy and peaks can be formed. Scrape down inside of bowl and cover with a damp cloth.

FLOWER PASTE

INGREDIENTS

Icing sugar (sieved)	455g (16oz)
Gum tragacanth	3 tsps
Cold water	5 tsps
Gelatine	2 tsps
White vegetable fat	2 tsps
Liquid glucose	2 tsps
Egg white	1 (size 2)

Flower paste is a firm, sweet paste which produces a life-like translucent finish, ideal for modelling flowers.

The paste dries very quickly so it is important to cut only a small piece at a time when using, and the bulk should be re-sealed. A small piece will go a long way when rolled out very thinly. Each piece of paste should be worked well with the fingers before use in order to achieve the right texture. If it is too hard or crumbly, add a little egg white and white fat to make it more pliable and slow down the drying process.

Storage: Place in a food-approved polythene bag and store in an airtight container in a refrigerator. Bring to room temperature before use.

1 Sieve the icing sugar and gum tragacanth into a bowl. Place bowl over a saucepan of boiling water and cover with a cloth and plate. Heat gently until sugar is warm.

2 Pour the water into a cup. Sprinkle on the gelatine and leave for 10 minutes until spongy. Place cup in a saucepan of hot water (not boiling) until the gelatine dissolves.

3 Add the white fat and glucose to the melted gelatine and heat gently until dissolved.

4 Separate the white from the yolk of egg and remove the 'string'.

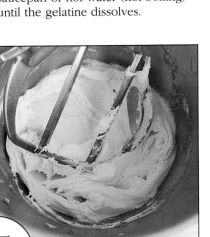

5 Add all ingredients to the warmed icing sugar. Beat for approximately 15-20 minutes until white and stringy.

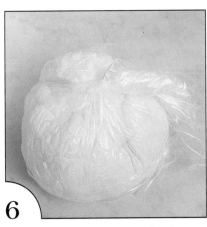

6 Place the flower paste in a food-approved polythene bag and store in a sealed container in a refrigerator for a minimum of 24 hours before use.

SUGARPASTE

INGREDIENTS

Water	2 tbls
Powdered gelatine	1½ level tsps
Liquid glucose	1½ tbls
Glycerin	2 tsps
Icing sugar (sieved)	455g (16oz)

Sugarpaste is a firm, sweet paste which is ideal for covering cakes. It can easily be rolled out on a board dusted with icing sugar and shapes can be cut from the rolled-out paste and used as decorations. The paste is also easily shaped with the fingers and this makes it ideal for hand-modelling animals, figures and flowers which will transform any cake into a work of art.

Food colourings and flavourings can be kneaded into the paste, but care should be taken that sufficient quantity is coloured to complete the project, as it is difficult to match colours at a later date. Food colourings can also be painted onto the paste after it has dried.

Storage: Sugarpaste can be made in advance and kept in a food-approved polythene bag in a refrigerator. It will keep for up to 2 weeks and, for this reason, the bag should be clearly labelled with the date it was made. Bring to room temperature before use.

1
Pour the water into a stainless steel or non-stick saucepan. Sprinkle on the powdered gelatine and dissolve over a low heat.

2
Add the glucose and glycerin and stir in before removing the saucepan from the heat.

3
Add the icing sugar gradually, mixing continuously with a wooden spoon to avoid any lumps developing.

4
Continue adding the icing sugar until it is no longer possible to stir the mixture.

5
Remove the spoon and add the remaining icing sugar by kneading the mixture between fingers and thumbs.

6
Continue kneading the paste until clear and smooth. The paste is then ready for use. See above for storage.

PREPARING AND COATING A GENOESE

1
Carefully remove the top crust from two genoese bases.

2
Place one base onto a cake board. Spread filling of choice evenly over the surface of the genoese.

3
Place the second genoese on top and lightly press to expel any trapped air pockets.

4
Place on a turntable and start to spread buttercream over the top.

5
Using a level palette knife, smooth the buttercream by rotating the turntable.

6
Spread buttercream around the side of the genoese, using the palette knife in an upright position.

7
Smooth the side with a plain scraper whilst turning the genoese on the turntable.

8
Remove surplus buttercream from the top-edge with a palette knife.

9
Place the coated sponge in a refrigerator for 1 hour. Repeat steps 4-8 or cover with sugarpaste (see p.22 steps 6-9).

COVERING CAKES WITH SUGARPASTE

1
Fill in any imperfections with almond paste and then brush the cake-top and sides with boiling apricot pureé.

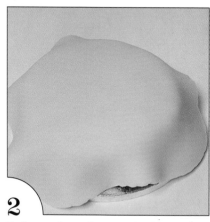

2
Roll out almond paste, dusting with icing sugar, and lay it centrally over the cake.

3
Rotate hand over the cake-top to smooth almond paste and expel trapped air. Gently smooth the almond paste around the cake-side.

4
Keeping knife blade close to the cake-side, trim away surplus almond paste from around cake-base. Leave to dry for at least 24 hours.

5
Brush the almond paste with cooled boiled water, or liquor of choice (see p.196).

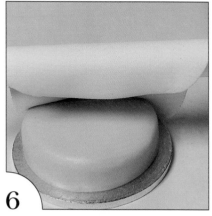

6
Roll out sugarpaste, dusting with icing sugar, and place it over the cake, lifting it with the help of a rolling pin.

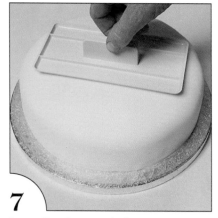

7
Immediately smooth the sugarpaste with the flat of hand and then polish with a cake smoother.

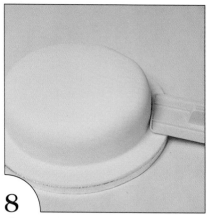

8
If required the cake board can also be covered with sugarpaste. This should be smoothed with a cake smoother, or by hand.

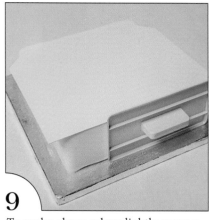

9
To make sharp edges lightly press a smoother onto the cake-top and then press and smooth up the cake-side.

CRIMPING AND RIBBON INSERTION

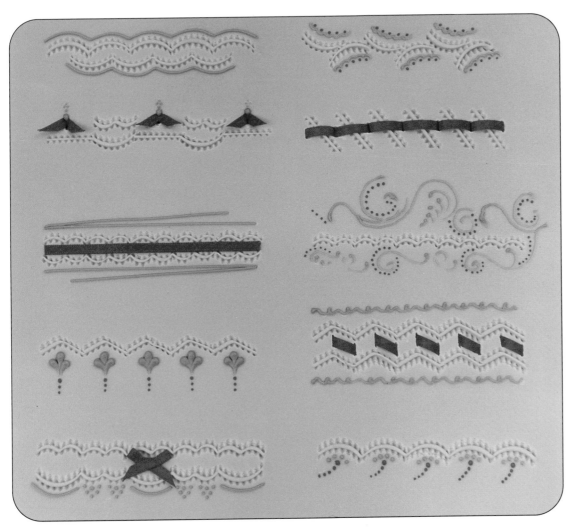

A variety of crimping patterns can be achieved from the different tools available.

Crimping can be enhanced with piped royal icing, ribbon insertion and bows.

1

Crimping: Cover a cake with sugarpaste (see p.22). Using a crimping tool of choice, immediately crimp the design required.

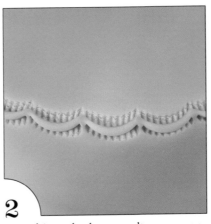

2

To achieve the best results, use even pressure on each crimp.

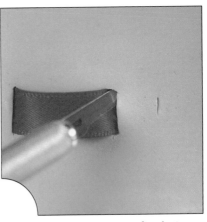

Ribbon Insertion: Transfer design to cake by cutting through a paper pattern. Push ribbon ends into slots with a sharp, pointed tool.

COVERING A ROUND CAKE WITH ALMOND PASTE

1
Remove the waxed paper and place the cake on a board. If required, brush on spirits and leave for 1 hour.

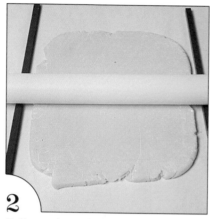

2
Roll out almond paste between spacers, as shown, using icing sugar for dusting.

3
Brush the cake-top with boiling apricot pureé.

4
Upturn the cake and place on top of the rolled out almond paste. Cut around the cake, as shown.

5
Upturn the cake once again and replace on the board.

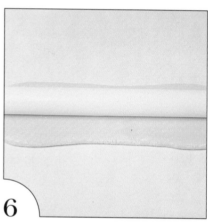

6
Using icing sugar for dusting, roll out almond paste into a long strip, wide enough to cover the cake-side.

7
Measure the strip to ensure it will cover the side in one piece. Spread a thin layer of boiling apricot pureé over the almond paste.

8
Fix the almond paste to the cake-side, using flat of the hand and trim off any surplus.

9
Leave the covered cake to dry for about 3 days before coating with royal icing.

COVERING A SQUARE CAKE WITH ALMOND PASTE

1
Remove the waxed paper and place the cake on a board. If required, brush on spirits and leave for 1 hour.

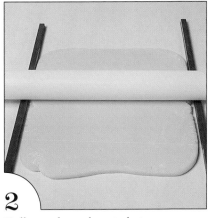

2
Roll out almond paste between spacers, as shown, using icing sugar for dusting.

3
Brush cake-top with boiling apricot pureé, upturn and place onto the almond paste. Cut around the cake and return to the board, right way up.

4
Roll out almond paste into a rectangle, to half the thickness of that used on the cake-top.

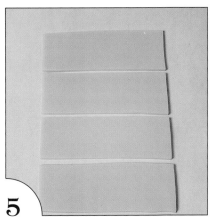

5
Cut the rectangle into 4 equal strips to fit the sides of the cake.

6
Spread a thin layer of boiling apricot pureé onto the strips, using a palette knife, as shown.

7
Fix the strips to the cake-sides, as shown.

8
Cutting towards the centre, trim away the surplus almond paste using a sharp knife.

9
Leave the covered cake to dry for about 3 days before coating with royal icing.

COATING WITH ROYAL ICING

Coating

Royal icing should always be coated onto an almond paste or marzipan-covered cake which has been allowed to dry thoroughly (see p.24-5). The icing should be made 24 hours before use as this allows the strength of the albumen to develop and will clear any bubbles to produce a smooth texture - freshly made royal icing is very fluffy and difficult to spread evenly. The introductory section to royal iced cakes on p.168 includes helpful hints for perfect results. For soft cutting royal icing, see the table on p.18.

There are two coating techniques which can be used, depending on whether sharp or smooth edges are required. The easiest and quickest method is to start with the top of the cake, spreading round and down over the sides and board in one operation, flattening and levelling as work progresses. This method produces a rounded edge. The method illustrated below is more time consuming but gives excellent results with the creation of sharp corners and edges, and is particularly suitable for formal designs such as wedding cakes. Whichever coating method is used, it is normal practice to coat the cake with three layers, the first layer being the thickest to take out any unevenness in the almond paste layer; the second layer being half the thickness of the first; and the final layer skimming the surface to give a perfect finish.

Colouring

If pale coloured royal icing is being used for coating, the first coat should be white, the second coat a pale shade of the colour required and the final coat(s) the actual colour. When strong colours are being used the first coat should be half-strength, the second three-quarters, and full strength for the final coat(s). Sufficient icing should be coloured to allow for coating all the tiers, as well as any additional icing that may be required for piping at a later stage, as it will be found to be virtually impossible to match the colour. When making royal icing in a pale shade such as lemon, do not add any blue as this will discolour the icing.

Drying

Whichever coating method is used, the quick or the careful, timing is important to ensure that the cake is perfectly dry and stable enough to be tiered at least two weeks before the occasion. A simple chart can be drawn up to indicate dates for covering with almond paste, time for coating and decoration. During adverse weather conditions, such as stormy, humid weather, drying may take twice as long. Drying cakes in an airing cupboard creates ideal conditions. Steamy kitchens and direct sunlight will affect the drying and the colour of the cake.

Tools For Coating

See p.168 for advice on tools.

Cake Sizing

When making tiered cakes, it can be useful to almond paste the cakes and then erect the tiers on pillars placed on thin cake cards, to check visually for correct proportions. If the top tier is too deep, it is easy to cut off the bottom of the cake at this stage.

Cake Boards

Always use thick cake boards for fruit cakes as otherwise damage can occur when moving. For single-tier cakes, it is usual to have the board 7.5cm (3") wider than the cake.

Tiering And Pillaring

See p.37 and the introductory section to wedding cakes on p.224.

1

To coat a round cake: Place cake on turntable. Using a palette knife, spread royal icing around the cake-side.

2

To smooth the icing, hold a scraper against the cake-side and revolve the turntable one complete turn. Repeat until smooth.

3

Remove the surplus royal icing from the cake-top and board, using the palette knife. Leave to dry for 12 hours.

4
Spread royal icing evenly over the cake-top using a paddling movement with the palette knife.

5
Level the icing by using a stainless steel rule in a backwards and forwards motion over the cake-top until smooth.

6
Remove the surplus icing from the edge of the cake-top and leave to dry for 12 hours. Repeat steps 1-6 for two more layers.

7
To coat straight-sided cakes: Coat opposite sides with royal icing, remove surplus. Leave to dry for 12 hours. Repeat on other sides.

8
Spread royal icing evenly over the cake-top using a paddling movement with the palette knife.

9
Level the icing by using a stainless steel rule in a backwards and forwards motion over the cake-top until smooth.

10
Remove the surplus royal icing from the edges of the cake. Leave to dry for 12 hours. Repeat steps 7-10 for two more layers.

11
To coat a cake board: Using a palette knife, spread royal icing over the cake board surface, as shown.

12
Smooth the royal icing, by holding a scraper steady, while revolving the turntable. Clean sides. Leave to dry for 12 hours. Decorate as required.

PIPING TUBE SHAPES

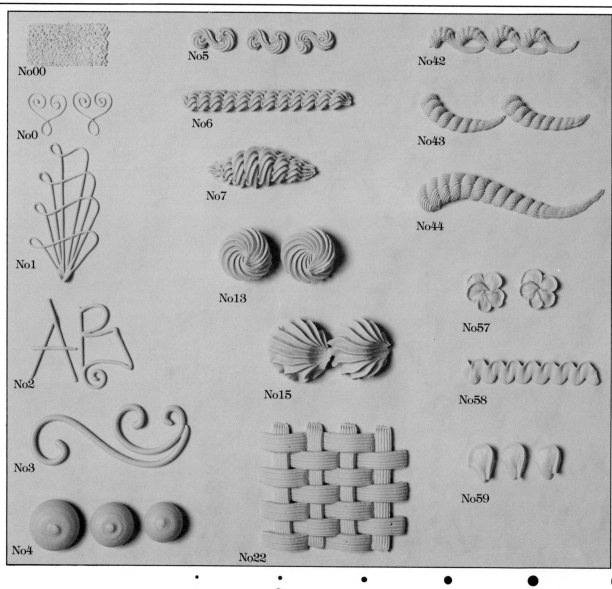

No00

No0

No1

No2

No3

No4

No5

No6

No7

No13

No15

No22

No42

No43

No44

No57

No58

No59

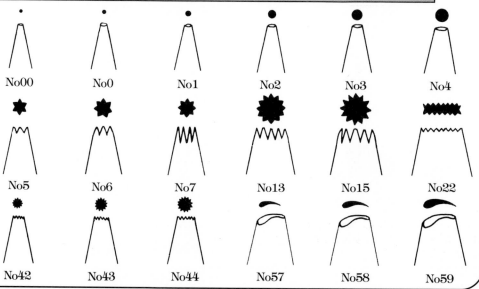

No00　No0　No1　No2　No3　No4

No5　No6　No7　No13　No15　No22

No42　No43　No44　No57　No58　No59

The above are Mary Ford icing tubes numbers for the shapes shown, but any comparable tubes may be used to complete the decorations in this book.

Note: As a rule, royal icing without glycerin is recommended for piping tube No's.00, 0 and 1.

MAKING A PIPING BAG

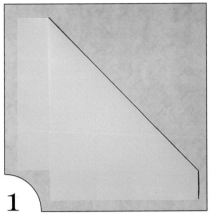

1 Size of greaseproof required: Large 45.5 x 35.5cm (18 x 14"); Medium 35.5 x 25.5cm (14 x 10"); Small 25.5 x 20.5cm (10 x 8"). Fold as shown.

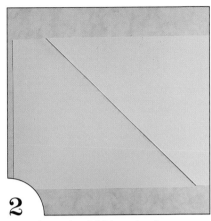

2 Cut along the fold line (to form two identical shapes).

3 Turn one piece of greaseproof paper long edge uppermost. Pick up the top right hand corner and start to turn it towards the centre, to form a cone.

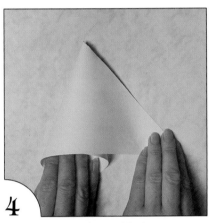

4 With the other hand, lift the opposite corner completely over the cone.

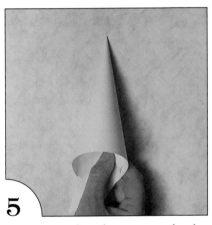

5 Continue curling the paper under the cone and pull taut, until a sharp point is formed at the tip.

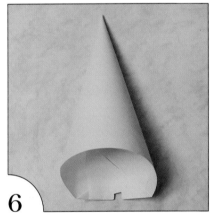

6 Fold in loose ends and cut and fold the small section shown (to secure the bag).

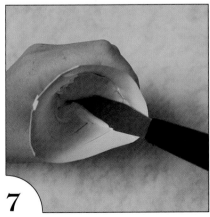

7 Cut tip off bag to hold a piping tube. Drop tube in and, using a palette knife, half fill the bag with royal icing or buttercream.

8 Flatten the wide part of the bag and gently squeeze filling down to the tube. Fold each side of the bag to the centre.

9 Roll the wide end of the bag towards the tube to seal the bag. It is then ready for use.

PIPED SHAPES

1

Star: Hold piping bag still in a vertical position and press. At required size, stop pressing and lift bag upright.

2

Rosette: Press upright piping bag whilst turning in a clockwise motion. On completion of one turn stop pressing and draw bag away.

3

'C' line: Pipe in anti-clockwise and upward direction. Form tail, stop pressing and slide tube on surface.

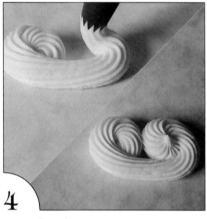

4

Lateral 'C' line: Pipe in anti-clockwise direction for first curve. Continue piping to form the matching curve. Stop pressing, lift bag upright.

5

Skein: Pipe an anti-clockwise curve. Continue in clockwise direction to form matching curve. Stop pressing and lift bag upright.

6

Reversed skein: Pipe a clockwise curve. Continue in anti-clockwise direction to form matching curve. Stop pressing and lift bag upright.

7

Shell: Hold piping bag at angle shown. Press to the required size. Stop pressing, then slide piping tube down along surface to form tail.

8

Zigzag: Pipe in tight waves whilst keeping piping tube on the surface. Continue piping an even zigzag. Stop pressing and slide piping tube away.

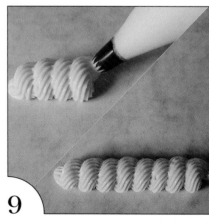

9

Rope: Pipe spring-shape in clockwise direction, using even pressure and keeping bag horizontal. Stop pressing and pull bag away in a half-turn.

10

Convex rope: Pipe curved spring-shape in clockwise direction, using even pressure, keeping bag horizontal. Stop pressing, pull away in a half-turn.

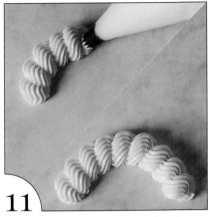

11

Concave rope: Pipe curved spring-shape in clockwise direction, using even pressure, keeping bag horizontal. Stop pressing, pull away in a half-turn.

12

Spiral shell: Pipe in clockwise direction, increasing the size of each circle then decreasing. Stop pressing, pull away in a half-turn.

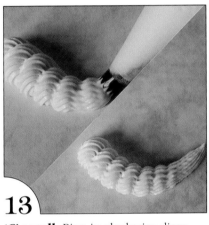

13

'C' scroll: Pipe in clockwise direction, increasing then decreasing each circle size, to form tail. Stop pressing and slide away.

14

Reversed 'C' scroll: Pipe in clockwise direction, increasing then decreasing each circle size, to form tail. Stop pressing and slide away.

15

'S' scroll: Hold piping bag at angle shown and start to press in clockwise direction, increasing the size of each circle to form body.

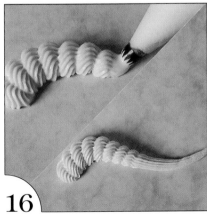

16

Continue piping, reducing the size of the circles from the centre. Then form the tail by reducing pressure during piping. Stop pressing and slide away.

17

Reversed 'S' scroll: Hold piping bag at angle shown and start to press in an anti-clockwise direction, increasing the size of each circle to form body.

18

Continue piping, reducing the size of the circles from the centre. Then form the tail by reducing pressure during piping. Stop pressing and slide away.

TEMPLATES AND DESIGNS

1

Where to find pictures: Select themes and illustrations from nursery rhyme books.

2

Choose seasonal drawings from appropriate cards, etc.

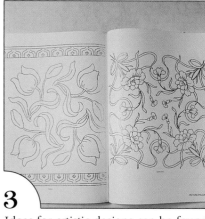

3

Ideas for artistic designs can be found in embroidery books.

4

Choosing the right size: Designs can be increased or decreased in size by using a photocopier. Picture shows template reduced to half size.

5

Picture shows the template in standard size.

6

Picture shows the template increased to double its size.

7

Checking the right size collars: Trace the picture or design onto greaseproof paper.

8

Glue the tracing paper, with the design, onto a piece of card and cut it out.

9

Place the card onto the cake-top to check for size.

10

Cut card templates: Trace or draw the design onto a piece of card.

11

Cut out all the sections, as shown.

12

Place the sections on the cake-top and pipe around each piece (No.1). Carefully remove each piece once the icing is dry.

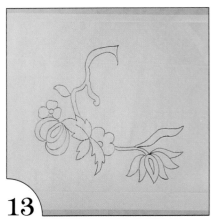

13

Tracing onto cake-top: Trace the template onto greaseproof paper using a food pen.

14

Place the tracing onto the cake-top. Using a sharp, pointed tool, press along the lines to leave an impression on the cake-top.

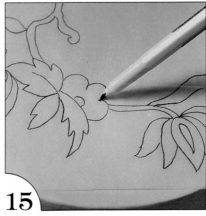

15

Alternatively, retrace the lines on back of tracing paper. Turn the paper over again and place on the cake-top. Trace again using a food pen.

16

Embossing: Trace the template onto tracing paper, as shown.

17

Lay glass, or an acrylic sheet over the tracing. Pipe over all lines in royal icing (No.1) and leave to dry for 12 hours.

18

Cover a cake in sugarpaste. While paste is still soft, gently press piped design into surface. Carefully remove the sheet to leave a clear imprint.

PIPING A CAKE

1

Picture shows a border piped too far in from cake-top edge, making the cake look small.

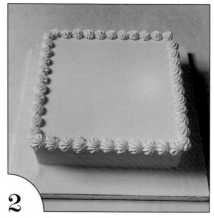

2

Notice how much larger and more effective the cake looks when the border is piped in the correct position.

3

The piping should be at an angle of 45° to the cake-top edge, as shown.

4

The cake will look top heavy if the cake-base is piped with a design which is too small compared with the piping on the cake-top edge.

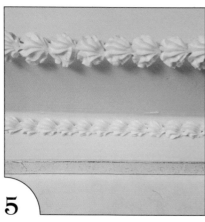

5

Do not pipe the border design too far away from the cake-base.

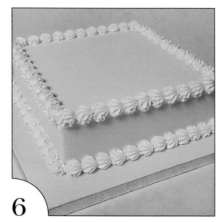

6

Picture shows piping in the correct proportions.

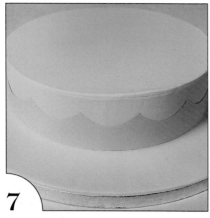

7

To pipe a line against the cake-side, make and fix a paper template as shown.

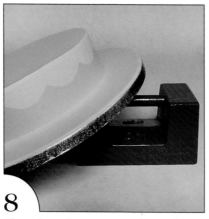

8

Place the cake on a non-slip surface, tilting and supporting it on a heavy weight or strong box.

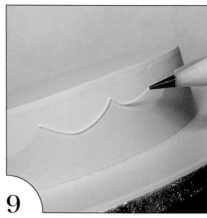

9

Pipe a line from top of curve, lifting tube away from cake-side to allow the line to drop. Finish by taking line up to next curve.

RUNOUTS, COLLARS AND FIGURE PIPING

1

Runouts: Make royal icing (without glycerin) 24 hours before use. Soften with cold water until it reaches a dropping consistency.

2

Draw design onto paper and secure to a flat surface. Lay a piece of waxed paper over the drawing and secure. Pipe outline in royal icing (No.1)

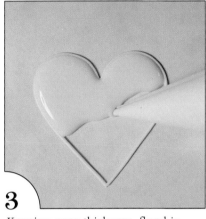

3

Keeping even thickness, flood-in outline, beginning at top and working from side to side towards the bottom. Leave to dry for 24 hours.

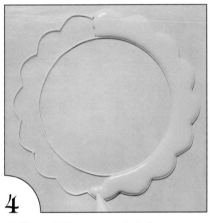

4

Collars: Follow steps 1-2 above. Flood-in the collar outline by adding icing at each end to avoid crusting, until the collar is completely filled.

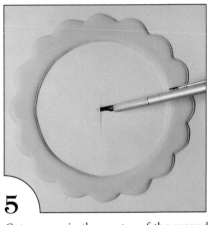

5

Cut a cross in the centre of the waxed paper to avoid damage from shrinkage. Leave to dry in a warm place for 24 hours.

6

Position the waxed paper with the dry collar over the edge of a table. Gently pull the paper downwards to remove collar from the paper.

7

Figure Piping: Repeat steps 1-2 without outline. Pipe in face, making cheeks and nose thicker and eyes more shallow. Pipe in neck and legs.

8

When the last areas are semi-dry, continue to fill in the figure, as shown.

9

Leave to dry for 24 hours. Paint in the face and other detail using edible food colourings before removing in the same way as for collars.

GARRETT FRILLS

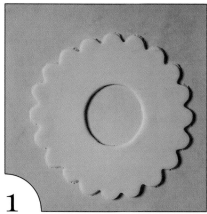

1

Dust the work surface with a little cornflour and roll out sugarpaste. Cut the shape, as shown.

2

Place the tapered end of a cocktail stick over the edge of the circle and rock it back and forth to create a frill.

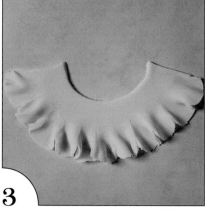

3

Cut the frilled circle in half, moisten with a little water and fix it to the cake, as required.

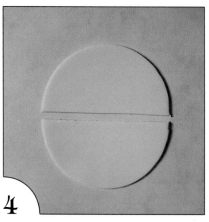

4

Cut a circle from rolled out sugarpaste and cut it in half, as shown.

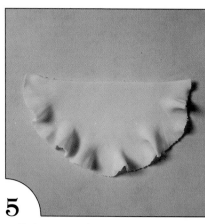

5

Frill the edge of each half circle as shown in step 2.

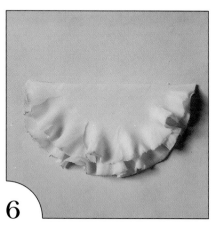

6

Moisten the straight edge of the half circles and fix one on top of the other.

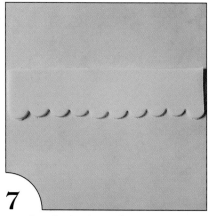

7

Cut the above shape from rolled out sugarpaste.

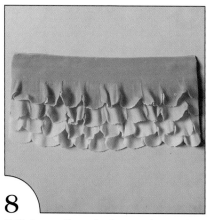

8

Frill the scalloped edge as shown in step 2. Repeat steps 7-8 as required. Moisten the straight edges and fix the layers, as shown.

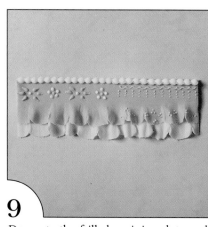

9

Decorate the frills by piping dots and small shells, as shown.

TIERING CAKES

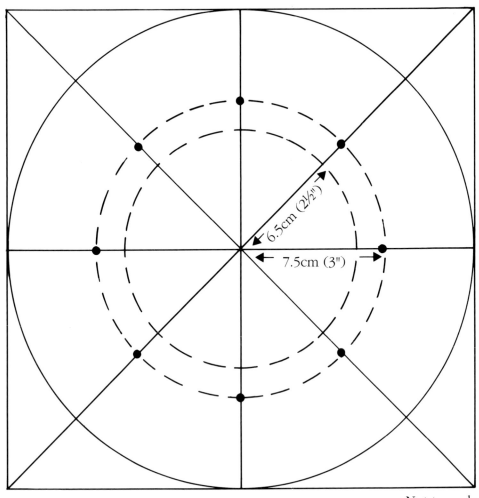

6.5cm (2½")

7.5cm (3")

Not to scale

For a 20.5cm (8") cake, pillars should be positioned 6.5cm (2½") from the centre. For a 25.5cm (10") cake, pillars should be positioned 7.5cm (3") from the centre. A square cake usually has 4 pillars which can be on the diagonal or cross, whichever suits the design best. A round cake usually has 3 pillars in a triangle.

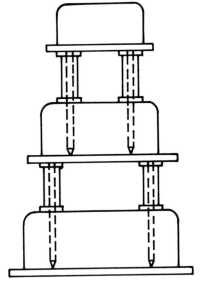

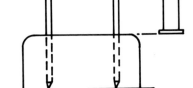 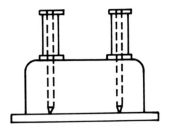

TIERING A SUGARPASTE-COVERED CAKE

1
Push food-approved rods into the cake to the board. Cut rods to height of pillar.

2
Place the pillars over the rods.

3
Assemble the cake, as required.

BUTTERCREAM

Buttercream is a quick, easy and versatile coating and decorating medium which is particularly appropriate for covering sponges and as a base for piped chocolate. It is ideal for creating novelty cakes as it can be spread, stippled or piped to create a variety of effects including filigree and flowers. The colour and taste of buttercream can be suited to the occasion and to the age of the recipient, which makes it very popular with young and old alike.

When colouring or flavouring buttercream, care should be taken to add a few drops at a time as artificial colourings and flavouring can be both strong and bitter. To add chocolate flavouring, melt the chocolate and warm the buttercream first in separate basins over warm water, and then beat the two together until well mixed. This avoids the chocolate setting and making the buttercream lumpy. Other ingredients, such as marshmallow, can be incorporated to vary the texture (see p.16).

The sides of a buttercream-coated cake can be decorated with toasted almonds, grated chocolate or combed with a scraper (see p.40)

to produce an interesting pattern. Decorative designs can easily be created in buttercream by piping a variety of shapes such as bulbs, shells, scrolls or lines. It is advisable to chill a buttercream-coated cake in a refrigerator for an hour before decorating as this makes the surface firmer to work on.

Filigree creates a very pretty finish and is easy to pipe. The buttercream should be slightly heated over warm water and then placed in a piping bag with a No.1 tube. Random 'M' and 'W' lines are then piped over the entire surface, or a lattice effect can be created by overlapping straight lines.

Buttercream is also an ideal medium for piping flowers, as the attractive cake on p.42 demonstrates. By using one or two colours of buttercream in a piping bag, a variety of flowers can quickly be created. The finished flower should be placed in the refrigerator and allowed to harden before handling.

Buttercream-coated cakes can also be piped with melted chocolate, as illustrated on p.40-41. Compound chocolate, such as chocolate drops or cooking chocolate, should be melted in a basin over warm water (or in a micro-wave for a few minutes until the chocolate has just softened). Stir well until the chocolate has completely melted, then remove the basin from the heat and slowly stir in approximately ½ teaspoon of glycerin per 225g (8oz) of chocolate, taking care not to add too much glycerin as otherwise the chocolate will become too thick. Piping chocolate can also be made by adding a few drops of water to the melted chocolate and stirring well. The chocolate should then be placed in a piping bag with the appropriate tube and used while still warm. Any additional chocolate can be kept warm over a basin of hot water. Alternatively, leaves covered in melted chocolate, or shapes and curls made from melted chocolate, can also be used to decorate a buttercream cake.

VALENTINE

1

Coat a heart-shaped sponge (see p.21).
Make and fix a sugarpaste ribbon
piped with inscription of choice (No.1).
Pipe shells around cake-base (No.7).

2

To make flowers, pipe bulbs of
buttercream (No.4). Pipe spikes over
bulbs (No.2). Dust with cocoa powder
and place in refrigerator until needed.

3

Decorate the cake-top edge with
scrolls and shells (No.7). Pipe stems
and leaves on cake-top and fix
flowers as shown.

CHERYL

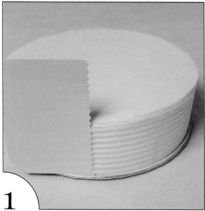

1
Coat a round sponge with buttercream (see p.21) and finish the sides using a comb scraper, as shown.

2
Cover approximately 2.5cm (1") of the cake-side with grated chocolate. Place the sponge on a doyley and chill in a refrigerator.

3
Using templates as guides, pipe 3 sizes of flowers in piping chocolate onto waxed paper. Pipe 6 small flowers using a bag without a piping tube.

4

Melt white chocolate over a pan of warm water. Flood-in each petal of the large flower with the melted white chocolate and leave to set.

5

Divide the cake-top into 6 and pipe the design shown in buttercream using a 6mm (¼¢") plain round savoy tube.

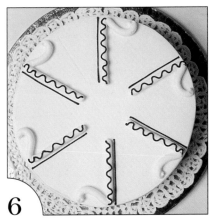

6

Using piping chocolate, pipe zigzag and straight lines, as shown.

7

Pipe a bulb of buttercream in the centre of the cake-top and fix the 3 different sized flowers, one on top of the other.

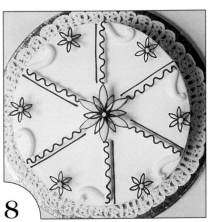

8

Pipe a bulb of buttercream in each section and fix a small piped flower to each bulb.

9

Complete the design by fixing half a cherry and a jelly diamond in the positions shown. Leave the sponge in a refrigerator until required.

TEMPLATES

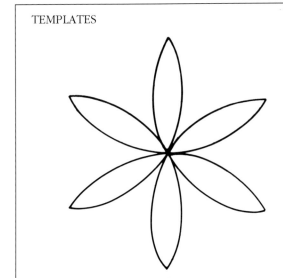

CLEMENTINE

1

Prepare and coat a round sponge with buttercream, as shown. Leave to cool in a refrigerator.

2

Using 2 colours of buttercream in a piping bag, pipe a rose centre, as shown with a large petal shaped piping tube.

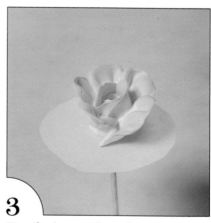

3

Pipe further petals to the rose, as shown.

4 Complete the rose by piping the outer layer of petals. Make 6 more roses in the same way and leave in a refrigerator to set.

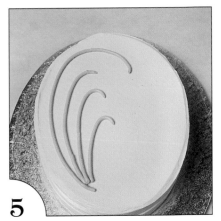

5 Pipe a series of curved stems onto the cake-top (No.4).

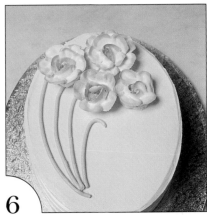

6 Remove the roses from the refrigerator and immediately place onto the cake-top.

7 Using a leaf bag (see p.102), pipe and fix leaves on the stems, as shown.

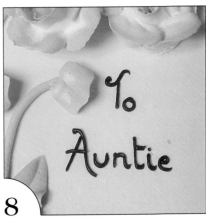

8 Using piping chocolate, pipe inscription of choice onto the cake-top (No.1).

9 Pipe a decorative border of rosettes and 'C' scrolls around the edge of the cake-top (No.13).

10 Pipe rosettes around the cake-base (No.13).

11 Pipe stems (No.4) onto the cake board and fix roses, as shown.

12 Using a leaf bag, complete the decoration by piping leaves between the roses.

HAMISH

1 Coat a square sponge with buttercream and cover sides with toasted flaked almonds.

2 Pipe design shown in buttercream (No.4). Pipe inscription (No.1) onto a plaque and fix to cake-top, together with jelly diamonds.

3 Pipe 'S' and 'C' scrolls in each corner (No.7). Complete the design by piping a rosette in each corner and top with a jelly diamond.

MODELLING

Sugarpaste and marzipan can be used to model a wide range of attractive figures and appealing decorations with a minimum of fuss and equipment.

These are ideal materials for decorating children's cakes, or for children themselves to work with as they enjoy the tactile experience of creating their own decorations - and eating them afterwards. With a little ingenuity and imagination, almost any item can be reproduced in sugarpaste or marzipan and these are ideal mediums for modelling children's much-loved toys, or father's favourite hobby. Nursery rhyme figures, delightful animals or fantasy items such as fairies or monsters from outer space will appeal to children of all ages and, as skill and confidence increase, more complex designs can be created. Both sugarpaste and marzipan are edible, although models made from either will keep almost indefinitely in a cardboard box around which air can circulate freely.

White marzipan is the most suitable for modelling as it can be easily coloured with paste food colours (liquid makes the marzipan too sticky) and commercial marzipan is easier to work with as it is not as sticky as home-made. If home-made marzipan is to be used, this should be made with ground almonds and icing sugar, not caster sugar, as this is easier to work.

Sugarpaste is extremely easy to use as it is pliable and does not crack. However, as it is very soft it is more suitable for simple figures. If a more complex shape is required, 2 level teaspoons of gum tragacanth should be added to each 225g (8oz) of sugarpaste, kneaded well and placed in a plastic bag for 2 hours prior to use. Alternatively, Mexican paste is equally suitable for models which require bulk. Where extra strength is required, pastillage should be used.

Continued overleaf

45

The figures should be stuck together with egg white, gum arabic solution, royal icing or melted chocolate as appropriate. Cocktail sticks or wires should never be used on creations for children's cakes, and must be avoided on any decorations which are intended to be eaten. If wires are necessary, they should not penetrate the cake covering but can be fixed into a small ball of sugarpaste to secure to the cake. It is also important to notify the recipient of the cake if wires have been used.

Before commencing work, the marzipan or sugarpaste should be coloured as required and placed in individual, sealed, plastic bags ready for use. It is important to have clean, dry hands and surfaces to work on. Icing sugar, or a mixture of icing sugar and cornflour, can be used to dust hands and surfaces to prevent sticking. It is best to work in cool, dry conditions as otherwise marzipan can become oily and moisture from hands will make sugarpaste tacky. Paste figures need to dry for 24 hours, away from direct sunlight, before fixing to the cake.

Modelling requires a minimal amount of equipment and many household items can be pressed into service. A small rolling pin, sharp knife, cocktail stick and a ball-shaped modelling tool may be needed. A crochet hook or knitting needle can also be used for shaping the paste if the proper tool is not available. Texture can be added with a cheese grater, sieve, etc.

Most of the basic shapes used in modelling can be created with the hands. A ball is produced by rolling a piece of paste between the palms of the hands, and this can be extended into a cone by rolling it between the base of the palms. To elongate the cone, it should be rolled with the fingertips along the pointed end on a work surface. To form a sausage shape, roll a ball on a work surface with the tips of the fingers. A ball tool is used to make indentations for eyes, etc. The easiest way to do this is to place the ball of paste in the palm of the hand and press gently with the tool. Cocktail sticks can also be used for indentations or to open up a shape, and will create a frilled effect when rolled backwards and forwards along a cut edge. Polystyrene or foam sponge may be needed to support the figure as it dries.

Once the basic figure has been made and dried for at least 24 hours, detail can be painted on with a fine paintbrush using liquid or paste food colour, or petal dust if a delicate effect is desired. Liquid colour should never be applied direct from the bottle as it may run. Instead, place a little colour on greaseproof paper, dip in the brush and wipe off any excess. If paste colour is used, this should be mixed on greaseproof paper and used in the same way. Colours should be allowed to dry before overpainting with another colour.

Sugarpaste can also be used to build up a picture in layers, as in the delightful Christmas scene on p.58. A sketch of the finished picture, preferably in colour, should be made and templates cut if required. This 'picture-book' technique can be adapted to any child, or adult's, favourite story or picture. The effect can be highlighted by piping and the thoughtful use of colour will enhance the finished effect.

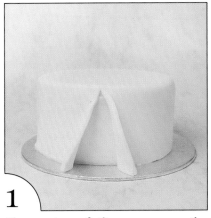

1 Place a piece of silicone paper on the side of marzipanned cake. Cover the cake in sugarpaste. Cut paste at paper centre, fold back, and remove paper.

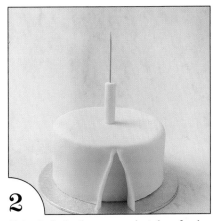

2 Trim kebab skewer, to height of cake, plus 11.5cm (4½"). Push skewer into cake to board. Slide roll of pastillage over skewer. Leave to dry.

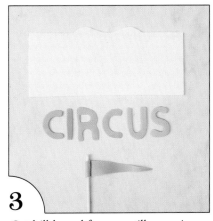

3 Cut bill-board from pastillage using template A. Cut out letters. Leave to dry 24 hours. Cut flag and fix to spaghetti. Support until dry.

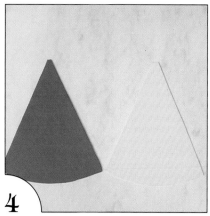

4

Using template C, cut 3 red and 3 yellow roof sections from pastillage. Leave to dry for 24 hours.

5

Colour almond paste to a dark grey and make a tapered roll, flattened at one end to form the sea lion.

6

Roll between fingers about 1cm (½") from blunt end to form neck. Mark neck wrinkles. Cut slit for mouth. Flatten sides, tail and shape flippers.

7

Cut tail and snip each side. Bend head and neck. Support until dry. Pipe eyes. Make second sea-lion, fixing a coloured paste ball to its nose.

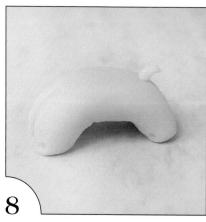

8

Make a long roll of almond paste. Snip ends to form legs. Bend into elephant body. Indent feet to mark toes. Fix a small cone for the tail.

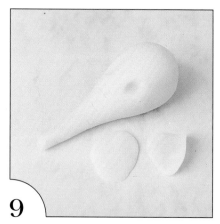

9

Make an elongated cone from almond paste. Indent eye sockets and score creases across trunk. Flatten 2 balls of paste for ears.

10

Fix ears. Indent end of trunk and bend to shape. Moisten underside of head and fix to body. Pipe eyes (No.1). Leave to dry 24 hours.

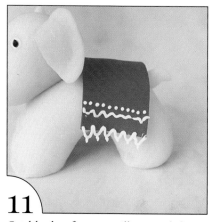

11

Cut blanket from pastillage and drape it over the elephant's back. Decorate the blanket edges with royal icing (No.1).

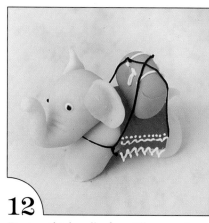

12

Form a thick roll of pastillage and flatten sides. Flatten base, smooth ends and mark lid. Leave to dry for 24 hours. Pipe lock and bands (No.1).

13 Mould a cone of almond paste and make a cut in the base to form clown's trousers. Smooth the cut edges and leave to dry.

14 Mould 2 almond paste hands. Using template D, make and fix coat from pastillage. Indent two 3cm (1¼") rolls of almond paste for shoes.

15 Indent sleeve ends and fix hands. Moisten underneath of arms and fix to sides of body. Moisten shoes and fix under trousers. Leave to dry.

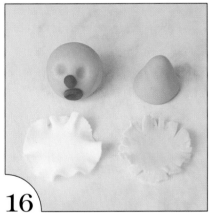

16 Indent eye sockets in almond paste head. Fix nose and mouth. Make pastillage hat. Using template E, cut collar and frill. Cut hair and snip.

17 Moisten collar and head and fix to the body. Fix hair and hat. Complete the clown by piping eyes, pom pom on hat, buttons and tears (No.1).

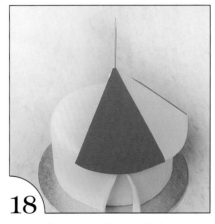

18 Fix roof pieces with royal icing, supporting as necessary while icing dries. Immediately remove skewer. Leave to dry for 12 hours.

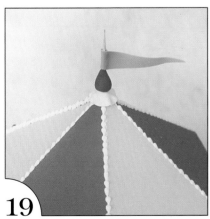

19 Pipe shells along roof joins (No.2). Fix spaghetti pole and flag to roof top with pastillage moulded shapes, as shown.

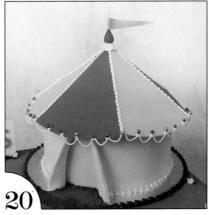

20 Pipe loops of royal icing around edge of roof (No.2). Fix circus tent to covered sponge. Pipe shells around base of tent and cake board (No.7).

21 Pipe inscription of choice (No.1) and fix small sugar flowers. Fix clown, bill-board and circus animals to the cake-top using royal icing.

TEMPLATES

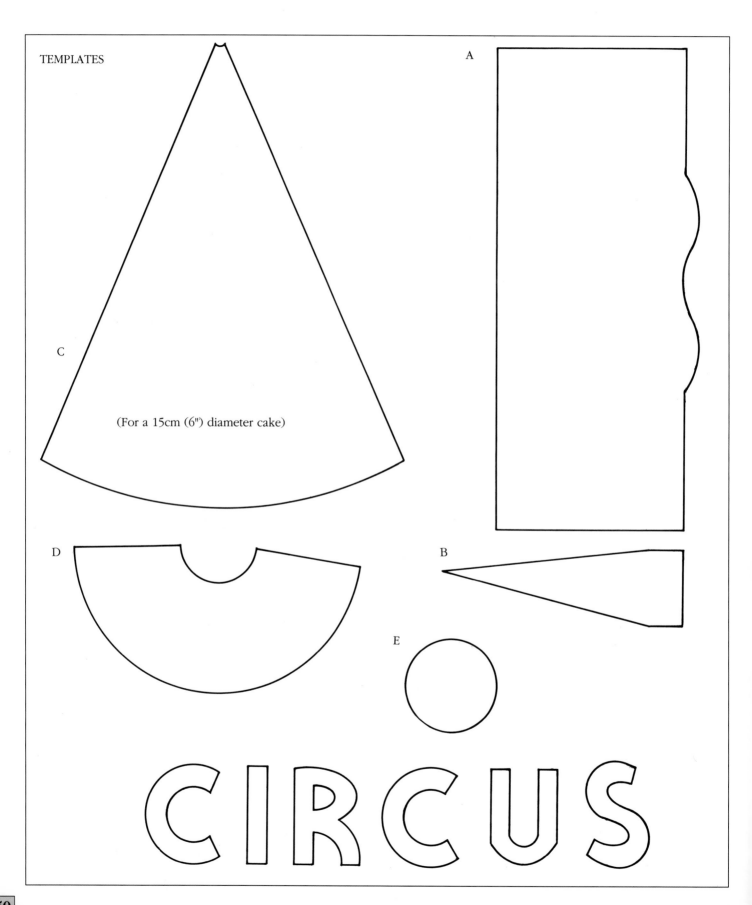

A

C

(For a 15cm (6") diameter cake)

D

B

E

CIRCUS

MISS MUFFET

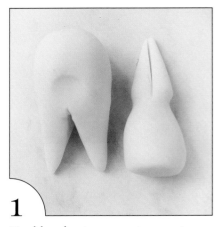

1

Mould and cut sugarpaste cone to form rabbit's body. Indent for head. Make a smaller pointed cone. Pinch to form neck and cut above for ears.

2

To shape ears, twist the cut pieces of the smaller cone forward. Indent the ears and form into points. Indent eye sockets, as shown.

3

Fix head to body. Pipe a tail and eyes in royal icing (No.1), then paint the mouth. (2 rabbits required). Leave to dry for 24 hours.

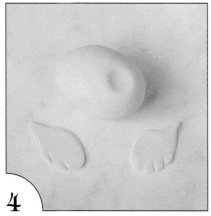

4

Mould a body from sugarpaste and indent for hen's head. Cut a pair of wings using template A, or leaf cutter, and mark with a cocktail stick.

5

Moisten and fix wings. Make a ball of sugarpaste for head and indent eye sockets. Make and fix cock's comb to head. Cut a small beak.

6

Fix beak to head. Pipe eyes in royal icing (No.1). Make 2 chicks in the same way as hen, omitting wings and comb.

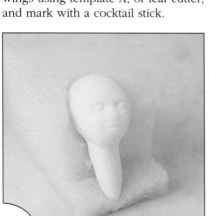

7

Mould head and neck of Miss Muffet from flesh-coloured sugarpaste, by hand or using a commercial mould. Leave to dry for 24 hours.

8

Colour the cheeks with dusting powder and paint the features with edible food colouring.

9

Make a cone from 22g (¾oz) sugarpaste. Make a hollow in the narrow end (wide and deep) to take the neck.

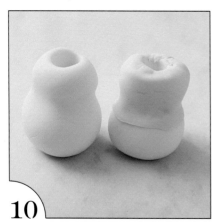

10

Mould side of cone to form waist. Cut a strip of flower paste for bodice, using template D. Fix to body, as shown. Leave to dry 24 hours.

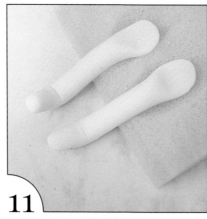

11

Make an 11.5cm (4½") roll of sugarpaste and cut in half to make legs. Indent ankles. Bend to form feet. Flatten tops. Support until dry.

12

Make arms and hands. Flatten tops, indent wrists and elbows before bending to shape. Make sleeve, using template E, and fix to arm.

13
Place a piece of almond paste or sugarpaste on the cake-top to create the tuffet before covering the whole cake in sugarpaste.

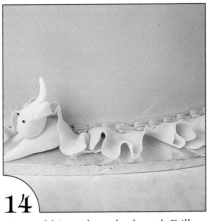

14
Fix a rabbit to the cake board. Frill and fix sugarpaste to cake-base. Pipe shells, using royal icing, around join (No.5). Fix a rabbit on top of the frill.

15
Paint shoes onto feet and leave until dry. Fix legs and body to tuffet using royal icing.

16
Cut out petticoat from flower paste using template B. Frill outside edge and snip round centre hole. Place over body and fix just below bodice.

17
Cut out skirt using template B. Frill outer edge and cut from waist to hem. Moisten body below waist. Fix skirt to petticoat with join at back.

18
Cover waist join with a ribbon sash. Fix arms and sleeves at shoulders (supporting arms in position until dry).

19
Pipe royal icing into the hollow of the body and fix head. Using template C as a guide, cut a collar and fix around neck. Pipe hair (No.0).

20
Make a slightly flattened ball of black sugarpaste for the spider. Pipe features in royal icing (No.1). Fix to cake-top and then pipe legs (No.1).

21
Make and fix sugarpaste blossoms to the cake-top. Pipe a centre to each flower (No.1). Pipe leaves as shown.

22 Arrange and fix further blossoms to the cake-top. Pipe a centre to each flower (No.1). Pipe leaves as shown.

23 Select and fix candle holders to the cake-top.

24 Pipe inscription of choice onto cake-side (No.1). Fix candles in holders. Make and fix bowl and spoon in Miss Muffet's hands, using royal icing.

TEMPLATES

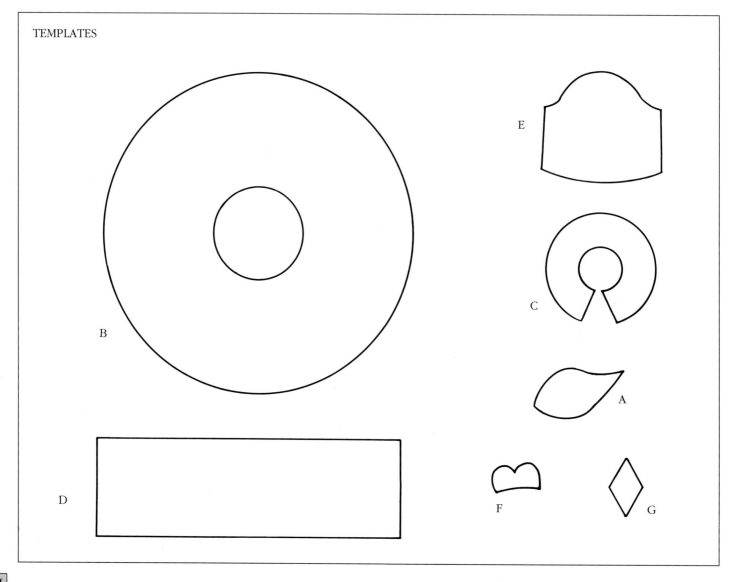

1 Layer an oval sponge with jam and buttercream. Cut 3 steps from one side, as shown.

2 Coat sponge with buttercream (see p.21) and place on board. Cover cake and board in sugarpaste. Smooth over steps. Indent side for rathole.

3 Use Mexican paste for all modelling. Mould a body, 6 legs, antennae, and shoes for a bug. Fix, as shown. Pipe eyes (No.0).

4

Flatten a paste ball. Mark turtle shell with No.3 piping tube. Make and fix feet, tail and head to underside. Cut mouth and pipe eyes (No.0).

5

Paint head and wings on a ball of paste to form ladybird. Make legs, bent at knees, and fix to underside of body. 2 required.

6

Pinch antennae in a paste roll for snail. Curl tapered roll of roughly coloured sugarpaste for shell, flatten end and fix to body. 2 required.

7

Make a short, fat roll of paste. Crease round middle to form woodlouse body. Make and fix hat and bow tie. Pipe eyes (No.0). 2 required.

8

Make 2 paste balls, one slightly smaller, then arms, legs and shoes for bee. Cut mouth. Paint stripes. Assemble then pipe eyes (No.0).

9

Form a roll of paste and mark segments with back of a knife. Curl and support until dry. 2 required. Make 1 small, white curled worm.

10

Form a tear-drop from paste for rat, and mark fur by scoring with a knife. Make and fix whiskers and nose. Pipe eyes (No.0).

11

Make a roll from paste. Pinch in about half way down and squash slightly to form toadstool drums. Paint when dry 3 required.

12

Cut 2 lily pads from rolled-out paste. Mark the veins with a cocktail stick and slightly curl the edges of one lily pad, as shown.

13
Flatten one end of a roll of paste for tree trunks and hollow out. Score with a knife to create bark effect. Brush on dusting powder, or cocoa.

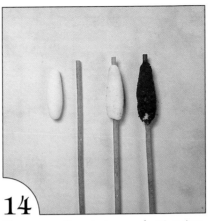

14
Fix cones of paste to spaghetti, using egg white, for bullrushes. Coat surface in egg white and dip into dusting powder mixed with semolina.

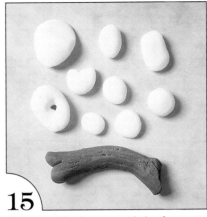

15
Score a roll of paste with knife to create bark effect on handrail. Dust with brown dusting powder. Make a number of sugarpaste pebbles.

16
Cut 3 star shapes from paste. Pinch and slightly curl up the edges. Fix together with egg white for lily. Leave to dry in dish dusted with cornflour.

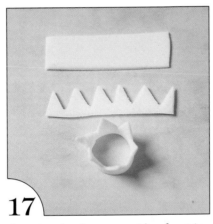

17
Cut triangles from one side of a strip of paste and fix into a circle, using egg white for queen bee's crown. Leave until dry.

18
Coat cake board with coloured piping gel and pipe shells around edge (No.2). Fix rat's head into hole and bullrushes in positions shown.

19
Cut strips of green paste and fix to cake-side. Fix pebbles, ladybirds and handrail. Lay lily pad on the water, with turtle and pipe reins (No.1).

20
Fix lily and second pad on the water, then the insects and tree trunk (with worm in hollow) to cake-top.

21
Make and fix drumsticks then fix bee's crown. Make, fix and decorate a double base. Make hats for worms and pipe eyes (No.0).

SANTA

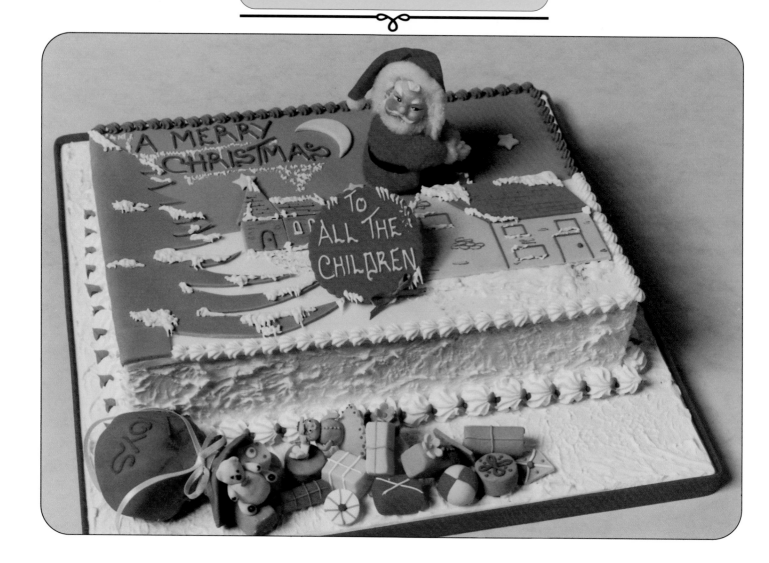

1 Cover a layered sponge with almond paste and 2 coats of royal icing. Stipple cake-sides and board. Cut sky and snow from sugarpaste and fix to the cake-top.

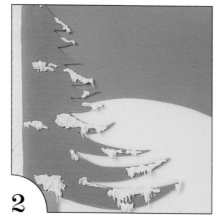

2 Cut fir tree from sugarpaste and fix to cake-top. Pipe royal icing onto tree to simulate snow (No.2).

3 Cut and fix a sugarpaste church. Decorate with royal icing (No.1) and paint detail with food colouring. Stipple pathway.

4 Cut the house, moon and stars from sugarpaste. Fix to cake-top, as shown. Pipe snow (No.1) and paint detail with food colouring.

5 Pipe shells along the edge of the cake-top where shown (No.5).

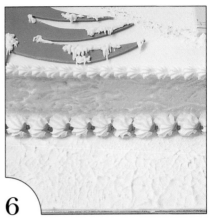

6 Pipe shells along the cake-base (No.7). Pipe leaves, using a leaf bag (see p.102), and dots in between shells (No.1).

7 Make a sack, together with an assortment of toys, from sugarpaste. Pipe detail in royal icing (No.1). Fix the pieces to the cake board.

8 Pipe Christmas message onto the cake-top (No.1). Decorate message with snow (No.1).

9 Cut a plaque from sugarpaste and fix to cake-top. Pipe inscription of choice (No.1). Fix a Father Christmas to the cake-top.

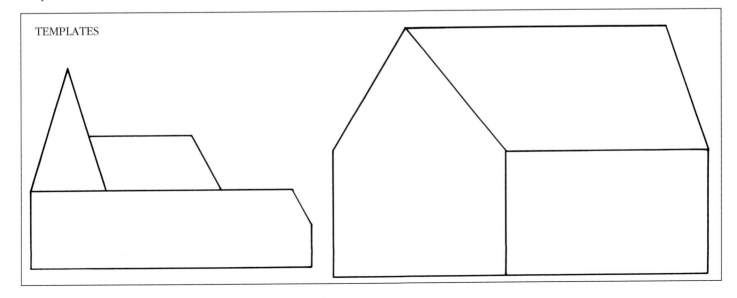

TEMPLATES

SILHOUETTES

Silhouettes were an extremely popular decorative art in the eighteenth century and were often found either painted directly onto the wall or hung in an ornate frame on a plain coloured wall. They were also used in place of family portraits prior to the advent of photography. The technique can be used to produce striking cake decorations as they look extremely dramatic when coloured in traditional black and white or, for a more subtle effect, in a dark and light shade of the same colour.

Many designs taken from magazines, or from Chinese or Japanese birthday cards, are suitable for the silhouette treatment and teenagers would be delighted by a cake featuring their favourite pop star - particularly if this was on a sugarpaste plaque which they could then keep as a decorative item in its own right.

An unusual birthday or anniversary portrait can be created by enlarging a photograph on a photocopier and then tracing this onto the cake or a plaque. Alternatively, a shadow thrown onto a piece of white paper can be traced around. The profile can then be reduced to the appropriate size on a photocopier. Similarly, portraits of favourite pets or animals can easily be copied to provide lasting pleasure for the recipient.

The technique is then a simple one of painting in the design with diluted food colour, adding additional coats until the appropriate depth of colour is acquired. The cake can be designed to create a suitable 'frame', or the plaque positioned on the cake-top and a decorative border added to highlight the silhouette.

CHRISTOPHER

1

Using the smaller template, cut a plaque from sugarpaste and leave to dry for 24 hours.

2

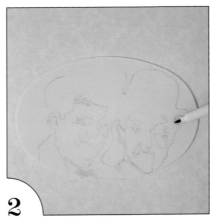

Trace the picture and transfer the outline to the plaque (see p.32).

3

Fill in the shaded areas by painting with food paste colour, diluted with alcohol. Two or three coats may be needed. Leave to dry.

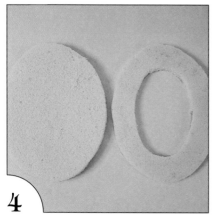

4 Slice the sponge in half. Using the larger template, cut an oval from one slice, as shown and remove the centre.

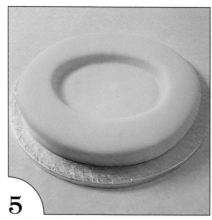

5 Sandwich together with jam and buttercream. Coat the cake in buttercream then cover in sugarpaste. Ease the paste into the hollow.

6 Place the dry plaque into the hollow. Fix ribbon around cake and board. Pipe around the plaque edge and cake-base, using royal icing (No.3).

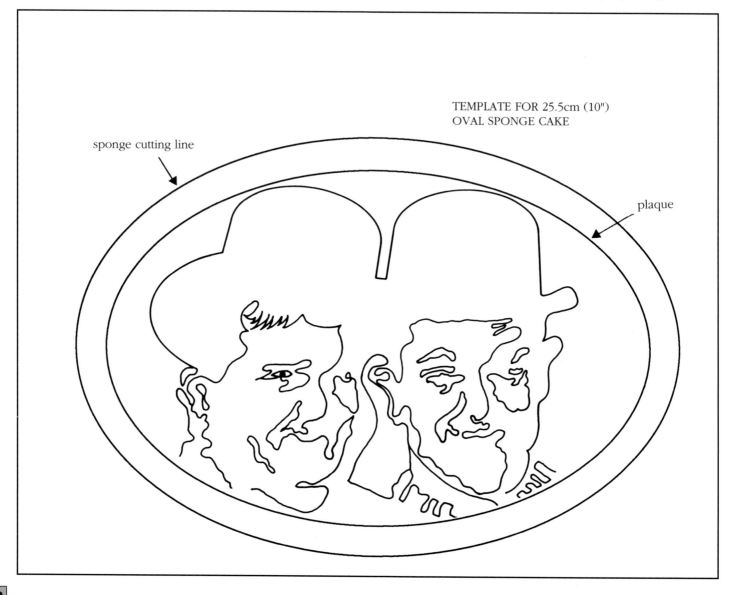

TEMPLATE FOR 25.5cm (10")
OVAL SPONGE CAKE

sponge cutting line

plaque

1 Using a suitable picture as a guide, draw an outline onto a cake-top or plaque with a food colouring pen.

2 Using black food colouring, paint in the birds and flowers with a fine paintbrush.

3 Complete the picture, ensuring that an even colour is maintained throughout.

4

Pipe inscription of choice onto plaque (No.1) and then fix plaque to the cake-top.

5

Filigree the remaining cake-top area, and then the board, using royal icing (No.0).

6

Pipe shells around the edge of the plaque (No.2), as shown.

7

Pipe a line over the shells (No.1). Overpipe the No.1 line (No.0).

8

Pipe plain shells around the edge of the cake-top and then around the cake-base, as shown (No.4).

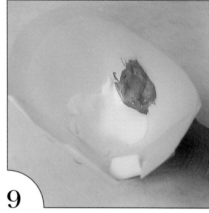

9

Fill a piping bag with 2 colours of royal icing with piping tube No.57.

10

Pipe a 'C' shape on top of each shell (No.57).

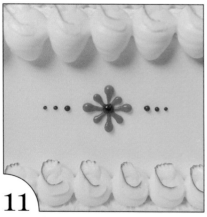

11

Pipe a decorative motif on each of the cake-sides, as shown (No.1).

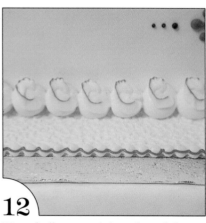

12

Pipe shells around the edge of the cake board (No.2) and then pipe a line over each shell (No.1).

RICE PAPER

Rice paper is a versatile decorating medium which is extremely easy to use and yet can create an elaborate centrepiece or a charming ornament on cakes for many occasions. Its simplicity makes it a favourite medium for children to work in as, with just a small amount of practice, they can quickly produce seasonal decorations such as Christmas trees, holly leaves and berries, coloured balls or Easter eggs and chicks. Rice paper, which has the added advantage of being edible and, therefore, particularly appropriate for children's cakes, can be used to create attractive place names or table settings as well as cake decorations.

Flat sheets of rice paper can be purchased from stationers or cake decorating suppliers. Rice paper has a smooth side and a rougher, more textured side, both of which can be easily coloured with a paintbrush and piping gel, or liquid or paste food colours, petal dust, edible inks, etc. Too much liquid should be avoided, however, as it does cause rice paper to disintegrate. Nevertheless, a small amount of water can be used to moisten the rice paper, which will then stick to itself without the need for glue.

No special tools are required for working with rice paper as it can easily be cut with a pair of scissors or a sharp knife. Basic, flat shapes can be drawn freehand or with the aid of templates. These shapes can then be folded or bent into their final form and fixed together where necessary. This technique can be used for anything from a flat, painted plaque to clothes for modelled figures or a sophisticated, three-dimensional model for the top of wedding cakes etc. Patience, imagination and ingenuity will soon create a masterpiece once the basic technique has been grasped.

Rice paper can also be moistened and roughly moulded into a solid shape with the fingers. Once the shape has dried, it will be extremely hard but can be trimmed with a craft knife. Children can use this 'papier mâché' technique to produce baubles and small figures, models, etc, without the need for trimming. Strong, primary colours will enhance the appeal of these gaily painted decorations, although subtle and delicate shading is also easily achieved and there is virtually no limit to the complexity of shape or colour that can be created with rice paper.

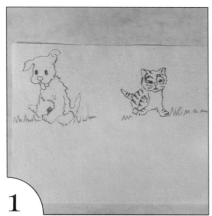

1 Using the templates as guides, draw the outline of the figures with food colouring pens onto the smooth side of rice paper.

2 Colour in the figures with dusting powder and pens. Draw the grass. Begin to cut out the figures and the grass, as shown.

3 Cut out the rest of the figures, taking care with arms and legs as rice paper is brittle. Cut out extra rice paper at each base for plinths.

4

Fix all the figures to the cake-top with piping gel. Write out a verse of the nursery rhyme on rice paper and fix it to the cake-side.

5

Cut out blossoms from sugarpaste and fix them to the cake-top.

6

Fix bows and blossoms to the cake and board using royal icing. Pipe inscription of choice on each corner (No.2). Overpipe inscription (No.1).

TEMPLATES

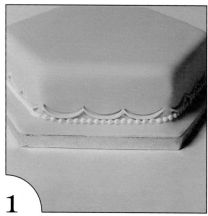

1

Cover, then crimp, a sugarpaste-coated cake, as shown. Pipe shells around the cake-base (No.2) using royal icing.

2

Using the template as a guide, draw the outline of the bear onto rice paper with a food colouring pen.

3

Colour the bear with dusting powder, highlighting areas to give a three-dimensional appearance. Leave to dry for 2 hours.

4 Pipe extension lines, as shown (No.1).

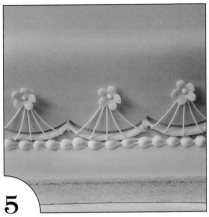

5 Make and fix small sugarpaste blossoms. Pipe in the centres (No.1).

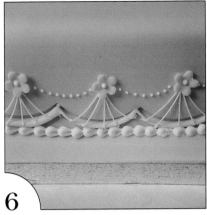

6 Pipe dots between each blossom to form loops (No.1).

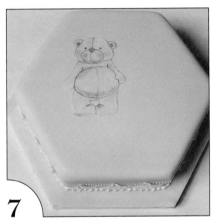

7 Cut out the bear carefully and fix to the cake-top with a thin layer of clear piping gel.

8 Make and decorate sugarpaste blossoms and fix to the cake-top, as shown.

9 Pipe inscription of choice and decorate with lines of piped scrolls (No.1).

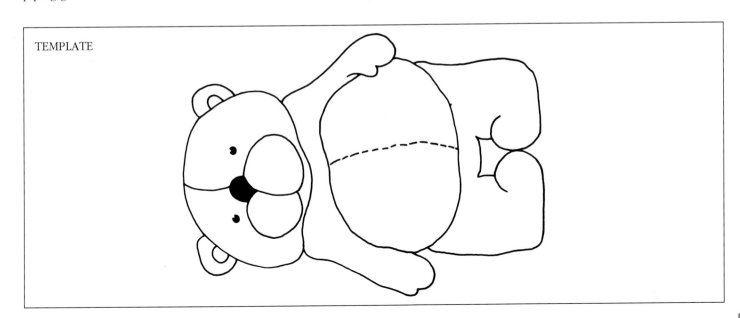

TEMPLATE

1

Using the template as a guide, trace the outline of the inscription onto rice paper, using a food colouring pen. Cut out as shown.

2

Coat back of rice paper with clear piping gel and fix to plaque or cake-top. Coat surface of rice paper with gel, brushing evenly in one direction.

3

Paint the inscription with food colourings. The gel coating will ensure that the colours do not run.

4
Fix to cake-top. Using brightly
coloured icing, outline and flood-in
the cake board design (No.2). Leave
to dry for 12 hours.

5
Pipe a series of scrolls and shells
around the cake-top edge and cake-
base, using royal icing (No.6).

6
Overpipe the scrolls, and complete
the decoration as shown (No's.2 and
1).

TEMPLATE

ROYAL ICING DESIGNS

Royal icing is the basis for many of the designs in this book. It can be formal and precise, with traditional piped shapes and sharp edges, or flowing and innovative as the attractive figures and decorative collars illustrate.

A little practice is all that is required to become proficient in the basic techniques and an imaginative mind will soon find ways of putting together the shapes in new and exciting combinations. Instructions are given on p.30-31 for piping the basic shapes and practice can be carried out on 'blank' cake shapes or on an upturned cake tin, and one of the easiest ways for beginners to master the art is to fill a piping bag with instant mashed potato as this can be used over and over again until confidence is gained.

The correct consistency of icing for each type of design is important and the introductory section to Royal Iced Cakes on p.168 sets out the consistency required for each type of icing. Royal icing designs can either be worked directly onto the cake or onto waxed paper and allowed to dry completely before being moved and assembled. It is useful to make extra pieces in case of breakage.

Basic Piped Shapes
Always pipe on a dry coated cake as any error can be scraped off. It is advisable to use two hands when piping. One hand exerts pressure on the bag while the other guides the tube. The angle and height of the bag above the cake and the movement of the hands will all help to form the finished shape. If over-piping, ensure that the previous piped work is dry enough to support the additional icing.

Star tubes are particularly versatile and will produce a variety of stars, shells and scrolls. Scroll borders, for example, can be built up by over-piping several layers as in the simple but extremely effective design on p.77-78. Plain tubes can be used to pipe designs, such as the bell on p.96 or seemingly complex lattices as on p.78, directly onto the cake, which are actually easy to work with a little practice. Plain tubes are also used to create lace, filigree or extension work, some of which may be attached to the cake at a later stage. If a pattern is required, this should be pricked into the cake coating before work commences.

Lace
Lace can be used to embellish many different celebration cakes and it can be combined with frills, extension or tulle work to form very attractive side decorations. The basic patterns for lace can be obtained from commercial lace, craft books, embroidery patterns or even wallpaper borders; or a motif from the bridal veil or dress could be reproduced. Pieces are normally about 2.5cm (1") long and sufficient pieces should be worked to allow for breakages. To work out how many pieces are required, measure the circumference of the cake and add between one-third and two-thirds as much again depending on whether the finished design curves or not.

The template should be fastened beneath a piece of perspex, glass, waxed paper or plastic (not cling film) and the lace carefully piped in freshly made royal icing using uniform pressure. The icing should be stiff enough to hold its shape but not so stiff that the lines break when piped. Any imperfections should be removed at the time of piping with a fine, barely damp sable brush. Once the lace has completely dried, it should be removed by very gently inserting a fine bladed knife under the lace and then carefully lifting it away. Lace is usually attached to the cake by two dots of royal icing, and the angle can be adjusted with a paintbrush handle or cocktail stick once it is in place. Attention should be given to equal spacing, and guide points can be pricked into the cake to ensure even curves.

Extension Work
Extension work, also known as curtain borders, makes a very striking decoration for cake-bases as in the design on p.216-218. The technique, which is worked in freshly made royal icing with a fine tube, offers scope for improvision and variation. The bottom edge of the border is usually scalloped but the top edge can be straight, curved, scalloped or

pointed and can incorporate lace or an appropriate motif for the occasion such as hearts or bells. To ensure even spacing of the scallops, it is essential to work from a pattern. Cut a strip of greaseproof paper the exact length of one side of a square cake or the circumference of a round cake, and the height of the border. Then fold the strip until the desired width of scallop is achieved and cut the bottom into a shallow curve. The top should be trimmed into the required shape or left straight as desired. Steps on p.219-20 illustrated the technique.

Filigree

Filigree is a delicate fill-in technique which should be worked in freshly-made royal icing with a fine tube. Step 2 on p.77 illustrates the technique which is based on continuous random piping of small 'M' and 'W' shapes.

Lettering

It is essential for cake decorators to develop a distinctive style of lettering and to practise this until it can be piped and spaced almost automatically with uniform height. Poor lettering can ruin the most beautiful design so it is well worth spending time to perfect the skill. A clear piece of perspex or glass should be used for practice and can be placed over a pattern if using a script for the first time. Once you have mastered the script, begin to practise common inscriptions such as 'Happy Birthday' until you become familiar with how much space each one takes up. You can then count the number of letters in a word and judge the amount of space a similar or slightly longer or shorter word would take up. If, for instance, the word has one letter less, you will know to start piping half way along the first letter of your practice inscription: if two letters less, start at the second letter. Once the association between the number of letters becomes automatic, you will always space the word correctly and will never run out of room. This technique can also be used to position a second word below the first line of an inscription. Inscriptions can be overpiped in a contrasting or toning colour, and may be decorated as appropriate, as on the cake on p.88.

Runout letters can also be used, following the technique outlined on pages 35 and 80, and positioned on the cake when dry to form the focal point of a design.

Runouts

Royal icing runouts can be used to create original cake motifs, such as the lions on p.82, or to produce an elegant collar to enhance a round or a square cake design. A soft peaking icing without glycerin is required for the outline and a runny consistency for the flood-in work. To convert royal icing for runout work, fold in sufficient cold water to achieve a dropping consistency. Where possible, the icing should be covered with a damp cloth and allowed to stand overnight to prevent bubbles spoiling the work. Before filling the icing bag, the container should be tapped hard to remove bubbles. It is recommended that pure albumen powder be used for the icing. The ideal surface for runout work is a glazed tile or a sheet of glass. Page 35 in the introductory section illustrates the technique. If more than one runout is required, these should be made at the same time and allowed to dry together to ensure a uniform finish. Dry runouts should be carefully removed from the waxed paper and can be stored in a box between layers of waxed paper until required.

Runout collars (see p.35 and p.74-75) are made using the same technique but must be carefully sized according to the diameter of the cake. Although the template can take time and skill to draw out, patterns can be used again and again so it is worth spending time on getting them exactly right.

Piped Figures

Piped figures, such as half-relief birds, (see p.246), are very popular decorations for cakes as they are quick and easy to make and need little expertise. Freshly made royal icing of a soft peaking consistency which holds its shape should be used. If the shaping is reversed for a second piece, the two halves can be fixed together to make a three-dimensional decoration.

LAURA

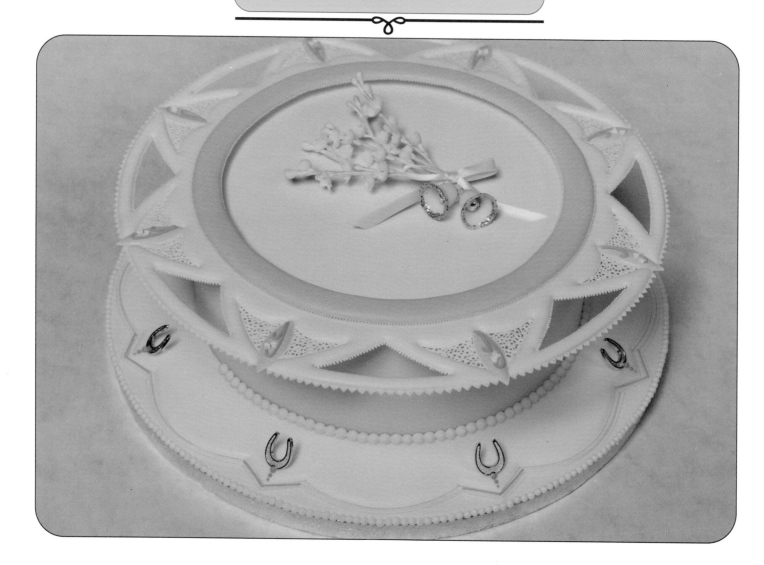

1 Using the template as a guide, pipe the outline of the design onto waxed paper (No.1) using royal icing.

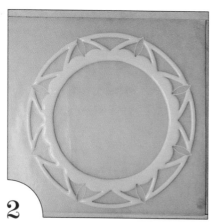

2 Flood-in the areas, as shown, using softened royal icing. Leave to dry for 12 hours.

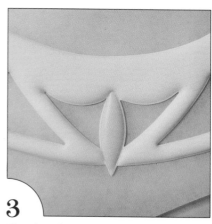

3 Flood-in the remaining oval areas of the design and leave to dry for 12 hours.

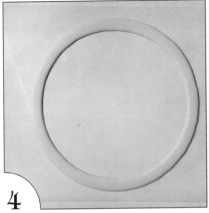

4 Using template as guide, pipe the outline of the dotted lines on waxed paper (No.1). Flood-in and leave to dry for 24 hours.

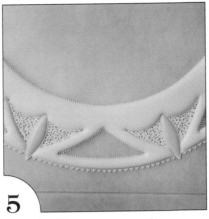

5 Pipe the filigree areas, as shown (No.0). Pipe dots around the outer edge of the design (No.0). Leave to dry for 12 hours.

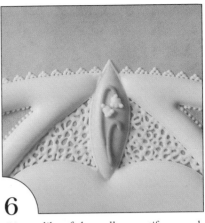

6 Pipe a lily-of-the-valley motif on each oval shape (No.1).

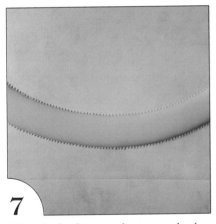

7 Pipe single dots, as shown, on both edges of the inner collar (No.0). Leave to dry for 12 hours.

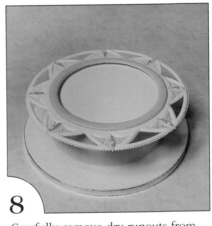

8 Carefully remove dry runouts from waxed paper. Pipe lines around the cake-top edge (No.3). Fix runouts to the piped lines, as shown.

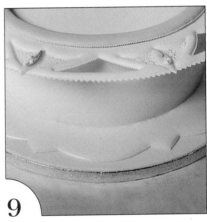

9 Pipe outline onto the cake board (No.2). Flood-in and leave to dry for 12 hours.

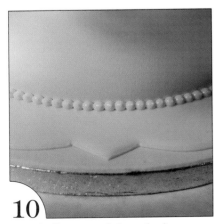

10 Pipe bulbs around the cake-base, as shown (No.2).

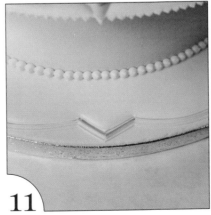

11 Pipe a line beside the cake board runout (No.2). Pipe beside and then overpipe the No.2 line (No.1).

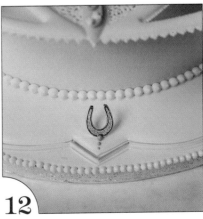

12 Fix decorations of choice to the board runout. Pipe graduated dots at the base of each decoration (No.1), as shown.

TEMPLATE

Note: Increase or decrease the template according to the size of the cake being decorated.

SOPHIA

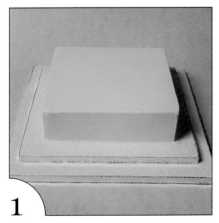

1 Coat a cake and boards with royal icing. Stipple each cake board surface. Filigree the cake boards (No.0) and fix band, as shown.

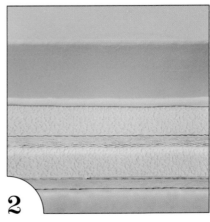

2 Pipe a line around the cake-base (No.43).

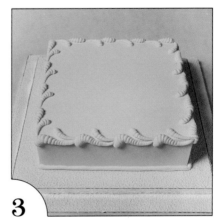

3 Pipe a series of 'S' and 'C' scrolls along the cake-top edge (No.43).

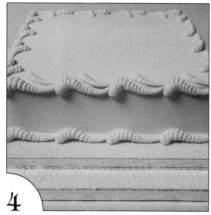

4

Pipe a series of 'S' scrolls around the cake-base (No.43).

5

Overpipe all the scrolls (No.3).

6

Overpipe all the scrolls (No.2). Pipe scalloped lines against the cake-sides (No.2).

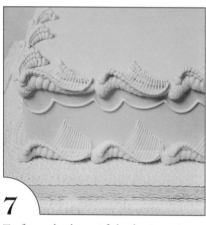

7

To form the base of the lattice, pipe lines above the scrolls around the cake-top edge and base (No.1), as shown.

8

Pipe lines in the opposite direction to complete the lattice (No.1).

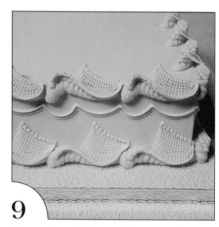

9

Pipe a line below and against the No.2 scalloped line on the cake-sides (No.1). Pipe shells along the top of the lattice (No.1).

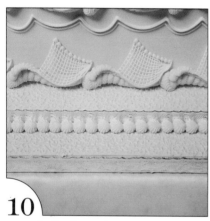

10

Pipe shells along the top cake board edge (No.43).

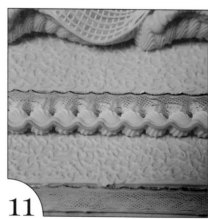

11

Pipe a line over the shells (No.2) and then overpipe the No.2 line (No.1).

12

Pipe inscription of choice onto the cake-top. Complete by fixing decorations of choice.

1 Using a stiff brush, lightly stipple a dry, sugarpaste-covered cake-top with food colouring.

2 Continue stippling down each side and out towards the edge of the cake board, gradually increasing the depth of colour, as shown.

3 Fix bands of ribbon, in graduating widths, around the cake-sides.

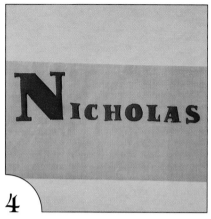

4

Outline (No.1) and flood-in the letters of the name onto waxed paper, using royal icing. Leave to dry for 24 hours.

5

Mould a tiny sugarpaste fish. Paint eye and dust with silver lustre. Make 5 sugarpaste daisies and leave all to dry for 2 hours.

6

Pipe inscription of choice onto cake-top using royal icing (No.1).

7

Using the template as a guide, pipe fishing line (No.00). Fix fish to end of line, as shown.

8

Using the template as a guide, pipe stems (No.1), then pipe leaves. Fix 3 daisies to the stem, leaving space for the initial letter.

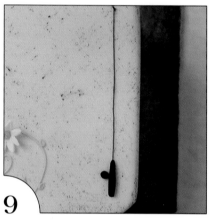

9

Pipe the fishing rod (No.1). Make and fix reel and handle from sugarpaste.

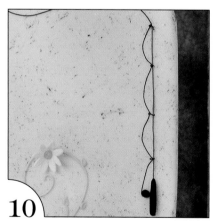

10

Pipe the fishing line and eyes along the rod (No.1), as shown.

11

Position and fix the initial letter and decorate by piping a curled stem (No.1) and fixing the 2 remaining daisies.

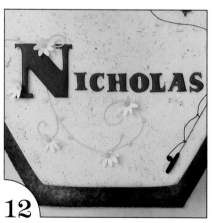

12

Complete the name by fixing remaining letters to the cake-top. Use a guide to keep letters straight.

TEMPLATES

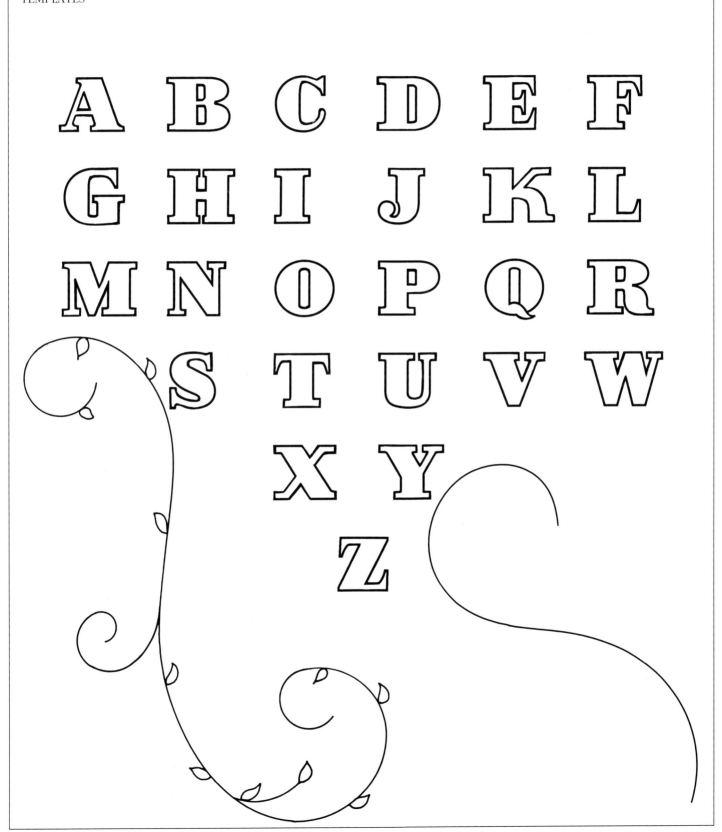

1 Using the templates as a guide, pipe the outline of each lion onto waxed paper (No.1) with royal icing.

2 Flood-in the outline with softened royal icing, as shown. Leave to dry for 24 hours.

3 Paint on the facial features, using edible food colourings.

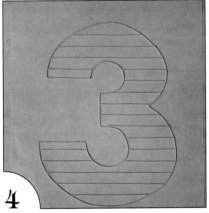

4

Using the template as a guide, outline and line the number (No.1) on waxed paper.

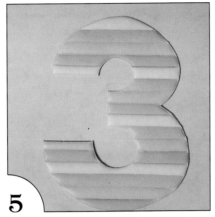

5

Flood-in the number with rows of different coloured softened royal icing. Leave to dry for 24 hours.

6

Carefully remove the dry runouts from the waxed paper and fix to the cake-top, in the positions shown.

7

Pipe inscription of choice onto the cake-top (No.1).

8

Pipe rosettes of royal icing around the cake-base (No.7).

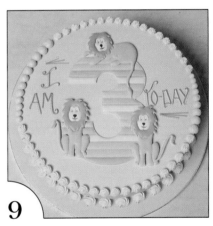

9

Pipe rosettes around part of the cake-top edge (No.7). Pipe the remaining cake-top edge with graduated plain bulbs (No.3).

10

Pipe pear-shapes around the edge of the cake board (No.3) between each rosette, as shown.

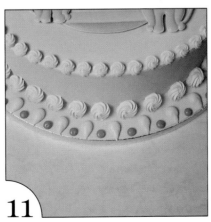

11

Pipe a bulb between each pear shape (No.2).

12

Decorate the cake-side with 3 different coloured ribbons, each 3mm (⅛") wide. Fix bows of ribbon, as shown.

TEMPLATES

NATALIE

1

Trace the template onto tracing paper, as shown.

2

Lay glass or an acrylic sheet, larger than cake, over the tracing and pipe over all lines in royal icing (No.1). Leave to dry for 12 hours.

3

Repeat steps 1-2 for the cake-side design.

4
Cover the cake in sugarpaste and, while still soft, gently press the piped design into the surface. Remove the sheet to leave a clear imprint.

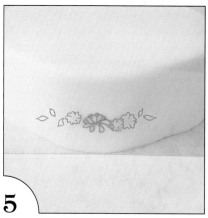

5
Press design into cake-side by gently rolling the sheet, (keeping lower edge on cake board) with even pressure. Leave to dry for 48 hours.

6
Flood-in the girl's neck and the boy's face using flesh-coloured runout icing. Brush out the wet icing at the boy's hairline.

7
Flood-in other areas in order: bodice, shirt, sleeves, collar, scarf, ear, hat and scarf knot. Pipe, then brush, boy's hair in royal icing.

8
Brush embroider the leaves (see p.188), starting with the background leaves.

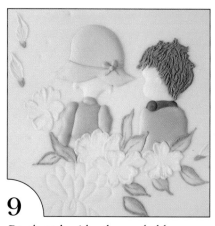

9
Brush embroider the apple blossom and buds, piping outer lines in pink and inner lines in white (No.0), as shown.

10
Brush embroider the peony. Pipe small flowers, stems, leaves and stamens (No.0).

11
Continue piping the small flowers and upright sprig (No.0). Paint girl's hair and boy's eyelash. Brush dusting powder onto boy's cheek.

12
Brush embroider side design in the manner shown.

13
Pipe inscription of choice on cake-top (No.0). Then pipe design around cake-top edge (No.0).

14
Fix ribbon around cake-side. Then pipe shells around the cake-base (No.5).

15
Fix ribbon and bow around centre of cake-side, as shown.

TEMPLATES

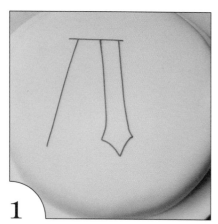

1 Using template as a guide, pipe the lines shown in royal icing to form the main letter (No.1).

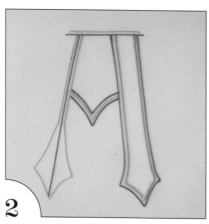

2 Pipe the further lines shown (No.1).

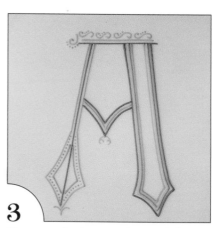

3 Decorate the letter with piped dots and tracery (No.0).

4
Complete the name of choice in the style shown (No.1).

5
Pipe curved lines against the cake-side (No.1). Then pipe a line below the No.1 line (No.0).

6
Pipe graduated bulbs around the cake-base (No.2).

7
Pipe curved lines around the cake board (No.2). Then pipe a line beside the No.2 line (No.1).

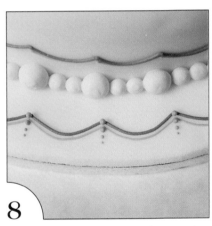

8
Pipe graduated dots at each curved line join, on the cake board (No.1).

9
Pipe the curved lines shown (No's.1 and 0). Fix decorative keys to complete the cake.

TEMPLATES

CONRAD

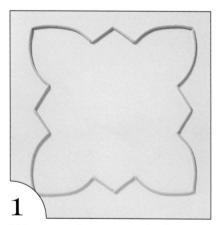

1 Make a template as a guide, then pipe the outline in royal icing onto the cake-top (No.3). Pipe bulbs around the cake-base (No.3).

2 Pipe further lines around the cake-top design (No.2), as shown. Pipe an 'S' scroll on each bulb around cake-base. Pipe a line around the board (No.2).

3 Pipe further lines around board and cake-top design (No.1). Pipe inscription of choice (No.1), fixing bows of ribbon and decorations as required.

PRUNELLA

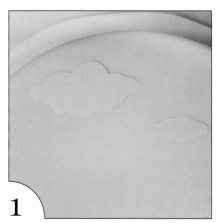

1 Using the templates as guides, cut out paper clouds and place on the cake-top, as shown.

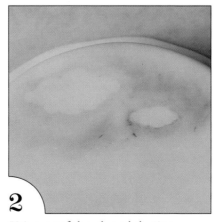

2 Using a soft brush and dusting powder, stipple the sky whilst holding the clouds in position.

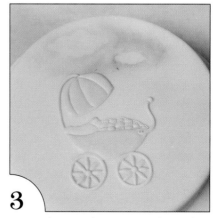

3 Using the template as a guide, make the pram runout and fix to the cake-top using a little royal icing (see p.35).

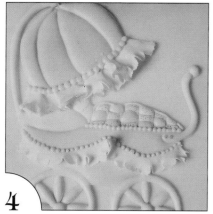

4

Make and fix sugarpaste frills (see p.36). Pipe dots (No.1), as shown.

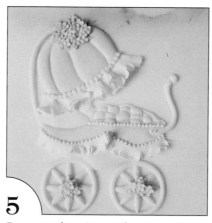

5

Decorate the pram with sugarpaste blossoms and piped leaves (No.1).

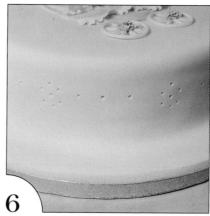

6

Push a sharp pointed tool into the cake-side to form holes in a regular pattern. Do not penetrate beyond the thickness of the sugarpaste.

7

Pipe a circle around each hole (No.0). Decorate cake-side with floral motifs and tracery (No.0).

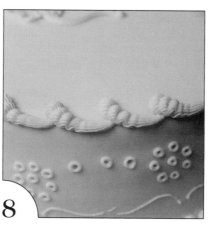

8

Pipe 'C' scrolls along two-thirds of the cake-top edge (No.42).

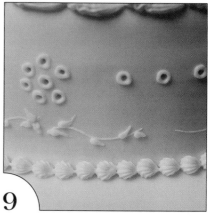

9

Pipe shells around the cake-base (No.42).

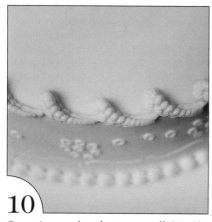

10

Overpipe each cake-top scroll (No.2).

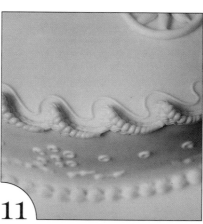

11

Pipe a line beside the 'C' scrolls (No.1) ending with a spiral (see step 12).

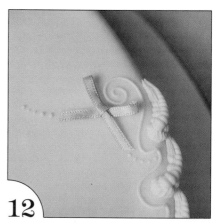

12

Decorate the first and last 'C' scroll with a bow and then pipe dots as shown (No.0).

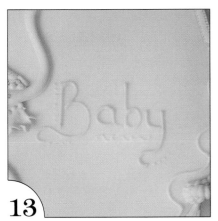

13
Pipe inscription of choice (No.1).
Decorate with piped dots and tracery
(No.0).

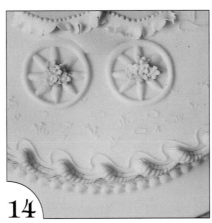

14
Pipe grasses and dots to form the
ground beneath the pram (No.0).

15
Pipe a scalloped line and dots around
the edge of the cake board (No.0).
Fix ribbon around cake board.

TEMPLATES

93

WITH LOVE

1

Using the templates as guides, outline the petals, hearts and leaves onto waxed paper with royal icing (No.1). Flood-in and leave to dry for 24 hrs.

2

Carefully remove the dry petals from the waxed paper and fix to the cake-top. Pipe the flower centre and stem (No.3).

3

Pipe further stems (No.3). Carefully remove the leaves from the waxed paper and fix to the cake-top, as shown.

4

Pipe inscription of choice onto the cake-top and decorate with piped bow motifs (No.1).

5

Carefully remove the dry hearts from the waxed paper and fix around the cake-base, as shown.

6

Pipe a bulb of royal icing around the cake-base, between each heart (No.3).

7

Pipe bulbs around the edge of the cake-top (No.3).

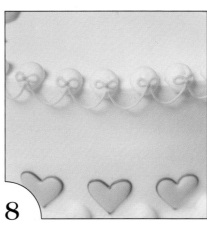

8

Pipe a bow motif onto each bulb around the cake-top edge, linking each with a loop, as shown (No.1).

9

Pipe graduated bulbs in the remaining areas around the cake-base (No.2).

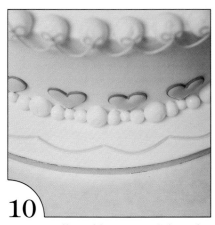

10

Pipe a scalloped line around the cake board (No.2) and then overpipe the No.2 line (No.1).

11

Pipe a second scalloped line around the cake board (No.1). Pipe bulbs around the cake board edge (No.1). Pipe a line over each bulb (No.1).

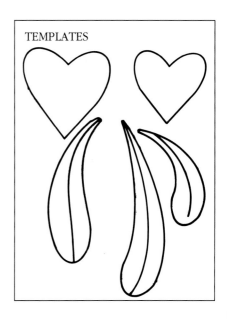

TEMPLATES

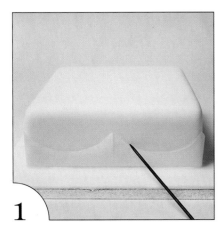

1 Make a template to the shape shown (see p.32). Using the template as a guide, score along the two curves on each cake-side, using a pointed tool.

2 Using template as a guide, pipe lines onto waxed paper (No.1) with royal icing. 64 pieces required for 20.5cm (8") cake. Leave to dry 2 hours.

3 Flood-in the top section of each design and leave to dry for 24 hours.

4

Using a non-toxic pencil, trace template. Trace again on reverse side. Lay tracing on cake-top, securing if necessary, and trace again.

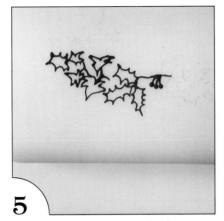

5

Remove tracing and carefully pipe over the design (No.1) using royal icing.

6

Continue piping over the design until the bell shape is completed.

7

Attach a ribbon, with matching bow, around the cake-base. Fix a ribbon around the edge of the cake board.

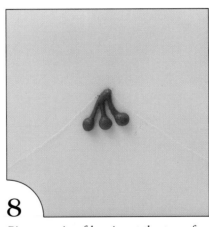

8

Pipe a sprig of berries at the top of each curve join, as shown.

9

Fix 2 lace pieces above each set of berries, as shown.

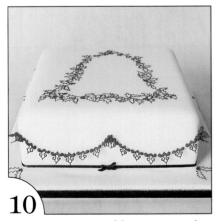

10

Fix remaining piped lace pieces. Alter spacing if necessary to ensure that an equal number of pieces are used on each side.

11

Pipe 2 holly leaves and 3 berries in royal icing on each corner of the cake board (No.1).

12

Fix 2 sugar doves (see p.246). Pipe graduated dots from the top of the bell out towards the cake edge (No.1).

TEMPLATES

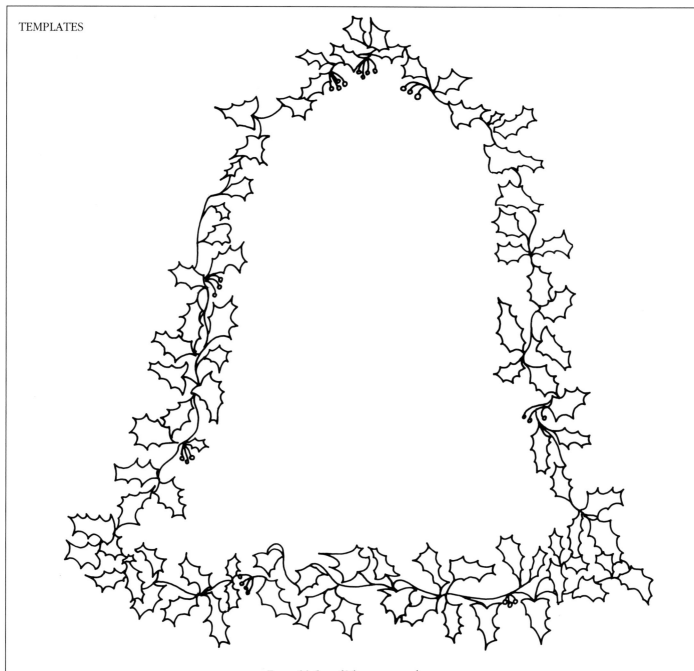

For a 20.5cm (8") square or larger.

Lace

HOLLIE

1 Using the templates as guides, pipe the angel's wing, candle and bow onto waxed paper with royal icing. Leave to dry for 24 hours.

2 Using the template as a guide, pipe in the parts shown onto waxed paper.

3 Pipe in further areas of the design, as shown.

4
Pipe in the remaining areas of the design. Leave to dry for 24 hours.

5
Pipe holly motifs onto the angel's dress (No.0) and then paint the wing with edible food colouring.

6
Complete the figure by painting in the facial features. Carefully remove the separate wing, candle and bow from the waxed paper and fix.

7
Pipe 2 circles around the cake-top (No.2).

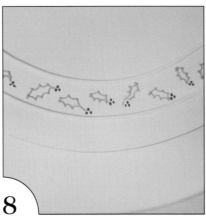

8
Pipe holly motifs onto the cake-top, between the piped circles (No.0).

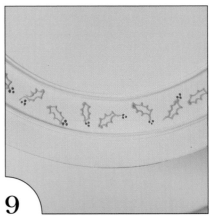

9
Outline the piped circles (No.1) and then overpipe the No.2 lines (No.1).

10
Fix the figure to the cake-top and then pipe the candle rays (No.1).

11
Pipe inscription of choice onto the cake-top (No.1).

12
Pipe 'C' scrolls around the edge of the cake-top, as shown (No.42).

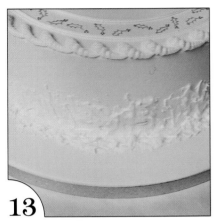

13 Spread royal icing around the cake-base and stipple to create a snow effect.

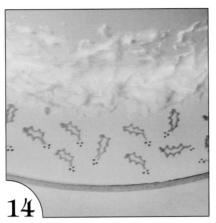

14 Pipe holly motifs onto the remaining area of the cake board (No.0).

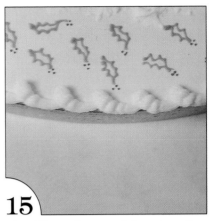

15 Pipe 'C' scrolls around the edge of the cake board, as shown (No.42).

TEMPLATES

A Happy Christmas

FLORAL ARTISTRY

Flowers are an extremely popular and versatile decorating medium for a wide variety of celebration cakes as they can be matched to virtually every colour and occasion. Piped in buttercream or royal icing, blossoms of any shape and size are quickly created, whilst modelling in flower paste, although taking a little longer, produces exquisite, life-like blooms to enhance any design. Sugar flowers will keep for years in an airtight box or glass dome, so brides can have their bouquets copied in sugar for their wedding cake and then have a permanent memento of the occasion afterwards. The colouring of flowers can be subtle and soft-hued, or vibrant and sophisticated and they will fit into almost any colour scheme and can be adapted to any size of cake.

Royal Icing Flowers

Royal icing flowers lend themselves beautifully to creating elegant and imaginative cake designs. These delicate creations are surprisingly practical too as, having no wires, they are completely edible (unless stamens are inserted), and particularly suitable for children's cakes.

Three-dimensional flowers, as used on the wedding cake on p.229, can be piped in advance and carefully stored in a cardboard box until required, whilst floral patterns can be piped directly onto the cake or onto a runout to enhance a formal design, as in the wedding cake on p.236. The stylish half-relief rose is particularly popular for wedding or anniversary cakes but a little experimentation will produce a flower that is suitable for almost any cake. Colouring a piped flower could not be easier. Icing of the appropriate colour is quickly tinted by adding a drop or two of edible food colouring to a small quantity of freshly made royal icing. The icing should be firm enough for the flowers to hold their shape but not too stiff, and additional icing sugar may need to be added to compensate for liquid food colouring.

A variety of piped dots, shells, lines and spikes can be used to form floral patterns for the top or sides of many cakes. Mixing flower heads with different shaped stems and leaves affords endless design possibilities and widens the scope of decoration.

Leaves are easily piped by cutting the tip off a greaseproof paper piping bag in a 'v' shape to the angle required. By varying the size and angle of the cut, small or large, broad or narrow leaves are produced and small flowers can also be created using a 'v' cut leaf bag.

Buttercream or chocolate can also be used to pipe flowers as the exquisite roses on p.42 demonstrate. Buttercream flowers, however, need to be put into a refrigerator to harden and chocolate should be kept in a cool place until set.

Flower Paste Blooms

With time, skill and patience almost anyone can create beautiful life-like flowers from flower paste and, with careful colouring, it can be difficult to tell the difference between a sugar flower and a real one. Patience is the most essential requirement as the drying process cannot be hurried and time must be given to experimentation and to copying flowers until the technique is mastered. Sufficient time should, therefore, always be allowed for in the timetable for preparing a celebration cake. When working with flower paste, it should be borne in mind that this medium quickly dries out and becomes unworkable. For this reason, it is best to use a walnut-size piece at a time, keeping the remaining paste in a polythene bag in the refrigerator until required. Thinly rolled flower paste produces the most realistic, translucent petals and the paste should be rolled out on lightly dredged cornflour or a thin layer of white fat to prevent sticking. Warmth affects the consistency of flower paste, as do moist hands, and in warm weather a slightly stiffer consistency is required than in cold.

Flower paste should be coloured with edible paste colouring. Add colour gradually, using the end of a clean cocktail stick, and then knead the paste until the colour is well mixed. The paste should then be returned to the refrigerator to chill. When colouring, always remember that red and yellow colours may deepen when left to stand. Alternatively, or in addition, fully dried petals and flowers can be dusted with confectioners' dusting powder or painted with a barely damp paintbrush.

Flowers can either be formed

from moulded cones of paste and then shaped as required (known as pulled flowers) or cut with a cutter. The pulled technique is ideal for filler or small flowers and was used for the violets on p.110. Purpose-made cutters, or cardboard templates, can be used to cut petals for larger or more complex flowers such as the carnations on p.106. If more than one petal shape is cut at a time, the extra petals must be immediately covered with plastic to prevent them drying out. When cutting, care must be taken to make a clean edge by using sufficient pressure. With the cutter upside down, a finger should then be run round the edge and the petal gently pulled out. If wire is to be inserted into petals or leaves, the base must be slightly thicker in order to insert the wire, and wires should always be moistened before insertion. Wires are available in various thickness and the gauge of wire required is specified in the step-by-step instructions. When making large, heavy flowers, it may be necessary to tape two or three thicknesses of wire together. Wires should never be inserted directly into the cake. A small ball of sugarpaste can be used to secure the flower, and all flowers should be removed prior to cutting. When assembling flowers, it can be useful to work over a large sheet of foam to prevent breakages. Fresh egg white, or gum arabic solution (1 teaspoon of gum arabic to 3 teaspoons of boiling water) is used for moistening. When instructed to moisten, this means to dampen the paste. Do not wet it or the petal will lose its shape.

A clean household sponge is useful for shaping petals, particularly if a ball-shaped modelling tool is being used to smooth edges or to form a cup shape, as in the freesia on p.108. This can, however, be carried out on the palm of the hand. It can be helpful to either very lightly dust the hands with cornflour to combat moisture, or to wear surgical gloves. Shaping techniques, such as frilling, should be carried out on a lightly dredged board.

There are many varieties of leaf cutter available and leaves can also be cut freehand to an appropriate shape. If leaf veins are required, these can either be made with a veiner or lightly scored with the end of a cocktail stick. The leaf should then be wired in accordance with the instructions given on p.105. Flowers and leaves require taping with florists' tape cut to half its width as this produces a much finer finish to the stem. The tape should be wound down the stem at an angle, the steeper the angle the thinner the finished stem. When completed, and fully dried, flowers can be used individually to decorate the cake or be formed into posies, sprays or vases.

Posies, Sprays and Vases
Floral posies are seen at their best on a round cake, or as table decorations. A mixture of round flowers with filler blossoms, ribbons and foliage will create an attractive posy or spray. It is important to work in a circular fashion as shown on p.116-117. Wrapping the posy in lace can provide a finishing touch, with the stems secured in a posy holder for insertion into the cake. Floral sprays are very popular for celebration cakes and should be carefully sized to the cake and a preliminary sketch prepared to work from. Sprays are also useful as place settings or to decorate the knife to cut a wedding cake. The technique is similar to that of posies. Large blooms should be positioned near to the focal point, which is usually towards the wider part of the spray, as on p.112. Remember not to crowd the flowers together as they are fragile and an airy spray shows off the blooms to the best advantage. A decorated vase can look very attractive as the centrepiece of a tall cake, as can be seen from the cake on p.229, or as a table decoration.

Silk Flowers
Copying fabric flowers can be an extremely useful way of practising sugar flowers, or experimenting with arranging flowers into sprays. They do however make striking decorations in their own right and silk flowers, in particular, can be extremely life-like. Most fabric flowers are wired on thick stems which need to be replaced by a much finer gauge wire in order to make them more flexible for arrangements.

Crystallised Flowers
Crystallised flowers are a useful way of decorating many celebration cakes as blossoms can be treated when in season (see p.244) and then stored in a cardboard box until required.

HYBRID ROSE

CUTTER SHAPES

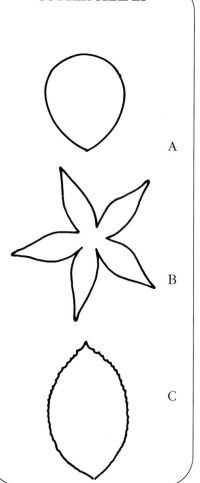

A

B

C

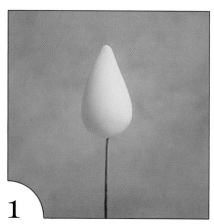

1 Mould a piece of flower paste to form a cone. Bend 26 gauge wire to hook shape, moisten and insert into cone. Leave to dry 24 hours.

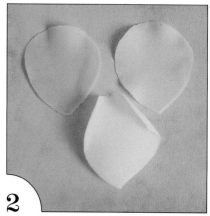

2 Mix pieces of paste to three shades of one colour, as shown. 7 dark, 3 medium and 5 light coloured petals are required, using cutter shape A.

3 Thin the outside edge of dark petal with a bone tool. Moisten and wrap dark petal around cone.

4 Moisten and fix 2 petals to each side of the first petal and interleave, keeping the top slightly open.

5 Repeat step 4 once more. Moisten and fix each petal to one side of the previous petal, keeping the tops slightly open.

6 Repeat step 4 once more. Moisten and fix each petal to one side of the previous petal, keeping the tops and sides open as shown.

7 Add 3 more petals, using the medium coloured paste. Equally space each petal around the flower, and then open out and shape as shown.

8 Add 5 more petals, using the palest colour paste. Equally space petals around the flower and open as shown. Leave to dry for 24 hours.

9 Mould a cone to form seed pod. Roll out white and green paste. Fix together and cut out calyx using cutter B. Cut edges as shown.

10 Moisten the centre of the calyx and insert the wire through the centre. Then moisten and fix seed pod as shown. Leave to dry for 24 hours.

11 Lightly dust the rose with confectioners' dusting powder using a clean, dry and fine artists' brush.

12 Roll out, cut and vein leaves using cutter shape C. Insert moistened 33 gauge wire. Leave to dry 24 hours then dust and varnish as required.

CARNATION

CUTTER SHAPES

A

B

C

1

(a) Twist 26 gauge wire around a stamen. (b) Mould a flower paste cone. Moisten joint and insert, shaping as shown. Leave to dry 24 hours.

2

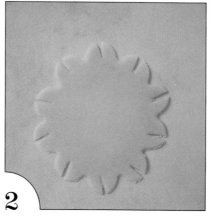

Using cutter shape A, roll out and cut petals from thinly rolled flower paste. Carefully cut each petal in half as shown.

3

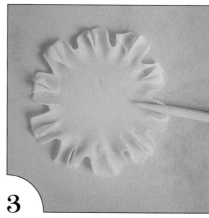

Frill the edges of the petal by rolling a cocktail stick backwards and forwards, a little at a time, until well frilled.

4

Moisten the centre of the petal and insert wire. Fold the petal in half and fix around cone as shown.

5

Moisten and fold the right side of the petal to the centre as shown.

6

Moisten and fold the other side of the petal to the centre back and gently shape to form centre of flower.

7

Repeat steps 2-3 to form another petal. Moisten centre and insert wire. Shape up around the centre to start forming the flower.

8

Repeat steps 2-3. Moisten centre and insert wire. Mould petal upwards to fan out beneath previous petals. Leave to dry for 24 hours.

9

Mould a cone to form a seed pod and, using cutter shapes B and C, cut 2 calyxes from thinly rolled paste.

10

Moisten wire and insert through seed pod. Moisten centres of calyxes and insert wire stem. Mould to shape. Leave to dry for 24 hours.

11

Carefully brush the petals with confectioners' dusting powder using a clean, fine and dry artists' brush.

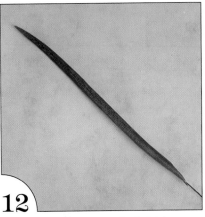

12

Cut a long, thin paste leaf. Moisten and insert 33 gauge wire. Shape leaf with a suitable modelling tool and then vein the centre.

FREESIA

CUTTER SHAPES

A

B

C

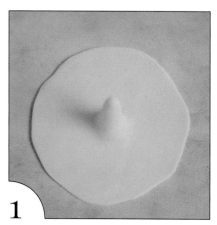

1

To make a flower: Make a cone from yellow flower paste and gently flatten the base as shown.

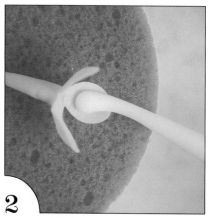

2

Place cutter shape A over the cone and cut. Smooth each petal to a deep curve.

3

Push a moistened hooked length of 24 gauge wire through the centre of the cone.

4

Roll out paste and cut another set of petals using cutter shape A. Smooth and shape petals, moisten and fix them into centre of cone petals.

5

Moisten and fix 1 long stamen and 4 short stamens into flower centre.

6

Roll out green paste and cut a small calyx using cutter shape B. Moisten calyx centre, insert wire and fix to the base of the cone.

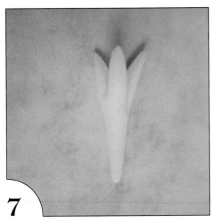

7

To make a closed bud: Make cone of flower paste, cutting it twice with a pair of scissors. Open out slightly to form 3 petals.

8

Twist the 3 petals together to complete the closed bud. Using cutter shape B, cut out, moisten and fix a calyx to the base.

9

To make an unopened blossom: Moisten and insert hook shaped 28 gauge wire into cone shaped paste. Make 3 grooves for petals. Follow steps 11-12.

10

To make a green bud: Form a cone of flower paste and insert a moistened hooked length of 28 gauge wire to make a bud centre.

11

Using cutter shape C, make a large calyx. Moisten centre, insert wire and wrap around the bud centre to almost enclose it.

12

Using cutter shape B, cut a small calyx, moisten and insert wire through centre and to base of bud.

VIOLET

CUTTER SHAPES

A

B

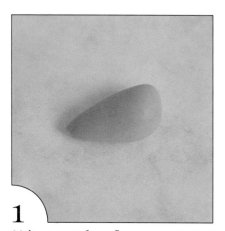

1 Make a cone from flower paste.

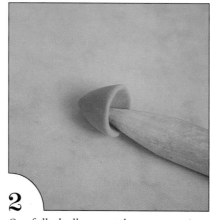

2 Carefully hollow out the centre using a cocktail stick.

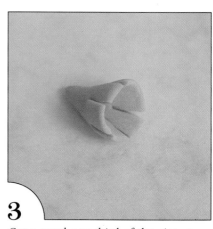

3 Cut a petal one-third of the circumference wide. Cut the remainder into 4 equal petals (5 petals in all).

110

4

Carefully open out all the petals as shown. Using a cocktail stick, make a small hole in the centre.

5

Using a bone tool, thin and shape the petals as shown. Curl the petals on either side of the large petal inwards towards the centre.

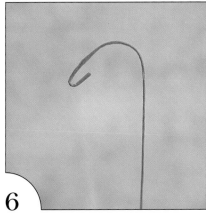

6

Bend a length of 26 gauge wire to the shape shown.

7

Moisten the wire and insert into top of flower. Moisten and insert a yellow stamen into the flower centre. Leave to dry for 24 hours.

8

Using a clean, fine artists' brush and edible food colouring, paint on the centre markings as shown.

9

Using cutter shape A, cut out a calyx. Make a cut to the centre as shown.

10

Moisten the centre of the calyx and insert stem. Mould the calyx around the flower as shown.

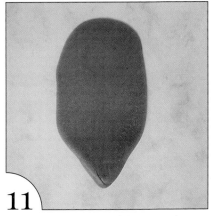

11

Cut a leaf freehand, following shape B, ensure that the paste at the base of the leaf is thicker.

12

Shape with a bone tool and vein with a veiner or a cocktail stick. Insert moistened 26 gauge wire into base of leaf.

1 Tape together 4 small sprays, each consisting of 3 buds and 2 pulled flowers. Tape each spray, as shown.

2 Assemble a rose bud (see p.104) with double ribbon loops, as shown. 4 required. Tape each spray, as shown.

3 Assemble 2 roses (see p.104-105) in full bloom, together with 3 double ribbon loops. Tape as shown.

4

Tape together 2 small sprays and form into a curve for top half of 'S'. Repeat, using remaining 2 sprays, curving in opposite direction.

5

Tape 2 rose buds to the top of the first spray and repeat in reverse for the bottom half.

6

Tape the 2 full roses to the first curved spray, as shown.

7

Tape the second curve to the full rose spray and make adjustments where necessary.

8

Bend the wire, as shown, to enable the spray to sit on the cake-top.

9

Picture shows completed 'S' spray.

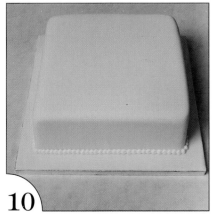

10

Cover a cake in sugarpaste and pipe royal icing shells around the base, as shown (No.2). Score each side to mark the position of the frill.

11

Make and fix a sugarpaste frill (see p.36) to one side, as shown, using a little cooled boiled water. Repeat for the other 3 sides.

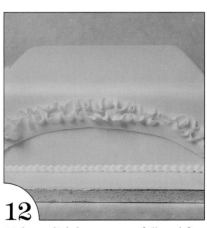

12

Make a slightly narrower frill and fix against the first frill, as shown. Repeat on all cake-sides.

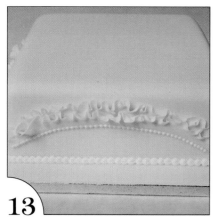

13 Pipe shells along the base of the frills, as shown (No.1).

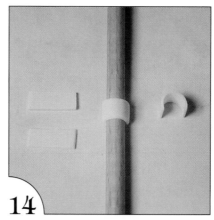

14 Cut very thin strips of sugarpaste to form ribbons. Cut into short lengths and dry over a piece of dowelling. Leave to dry for 12 hours.

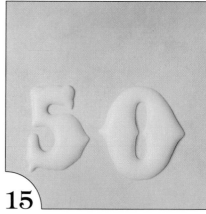

15 Using royal icing, outline and flood-in the numbers (No.1) onto waxed paper. Leave to dry for 2 hours.

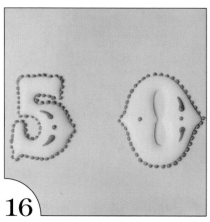

16 Decorate the runout numbers with dots of royal icing, as shown (No.1). Leave to dry for 24 hours.

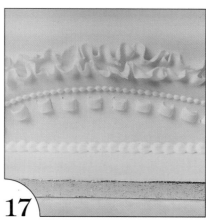

17 Cut slits in the sugarpaste, equal distances apart, beneath the frills. Insert the dry paste 'ribbon' pieces.

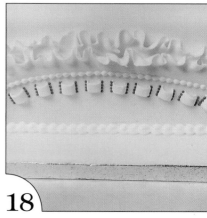

18 Decorate the 'ribbon' inserts with piped dots (No.1), as shown.

19 Fix the spray of flowers to the cake-top, using royal icing.

20 Fix the runout numbers to the cake-top, using royal icing, as shown.

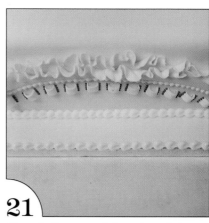

21 Pipe shells around the edge of the cake board (No.2).

FLORENCE

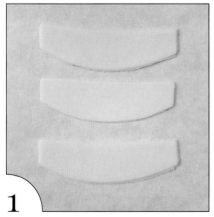

1

Using template A, or a cutter, cut out bridge sections in flower paste. Check length of each side of cake, and trim bridge sections if necessary.

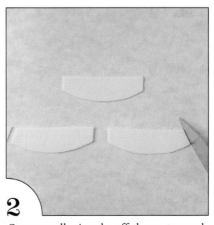

2

Cut a small triangle off the outer end pieces of each side to prevent the corners from breaking when pushed into the cake. Leave to dry 24 hours.

3

Using template B, pipe 60 pieces of lace onto waxed paper, and 6 corner lace pieces of C, in royal icing (No.0). Leave to dry 24 hrs.

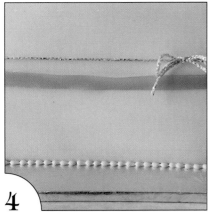

4 Scratch straight lines onto cake-side, 0.6cm (¼") and 4cm (1½") from cake-base. Fix ribbon and cord. Pipe shells around cake-base (No.1).

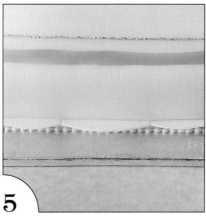

5 24 hours after covering the cake, push the bridge sections into the cake-sides, using lower scratch line as a guide. Keep sections level.

6 Pipe a line around the cake-top (No.2). Pipe a second line beside the No.2 line (No.1). Fix corner lace pieces, as shown.

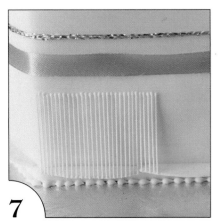

7 Pipe lace extensions, as shown (No.0), working from the higher scratch line to the bridge sections.

8 To neaten, pipe tiny plain shells against the edge of the bridge sections (No.0).

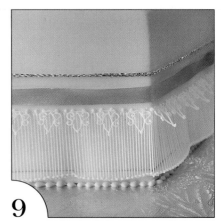

9 Carefully lift each piece of piped border lace from the waxed paper and fix to the cake-side, as shown.

10 Make 6 sprays of freesias, 6 roses, 6 rose buds, 9 hyacinths and 8 hyacinth buds from flower paste.

11 Make 18 small finger loops of ribbon and 6 larger double tail loops, as shown.

12 Tape hyacinths and roses, using 2 finger loops. Tape 6 sprays. Bend stem of last flower at right angles, just below last flower head.

13 Wire 3 hyacinths and 2 buds into a cluster. Add 10cm (4") of 24 gauge wire to strengthen and lengthen the stem. Tape down length of the stem.

14 Tape 5 or 6 finger loops around hyacinth cluster, holding tape at right angles to the wire, as shown to form the main stem.

15 Bend a freesia spray stem 90° just below the last flower. Tape to the main stem. Repeat 5 times, spacing the sprays evenly.

16 Tape 6 rose and hyacinth sprays between freesia sprays, as described in step 15.

17 Tape in 6-8 large ribbon loops below the last row of taping. Tape down stem to 2cm (¾") below the ribbon loops.

18 Cut wires 4cm (1½") below taped section. Spread into 3, trim and cover with tape. Bend at right angles. Arrange and fix on cake-top.

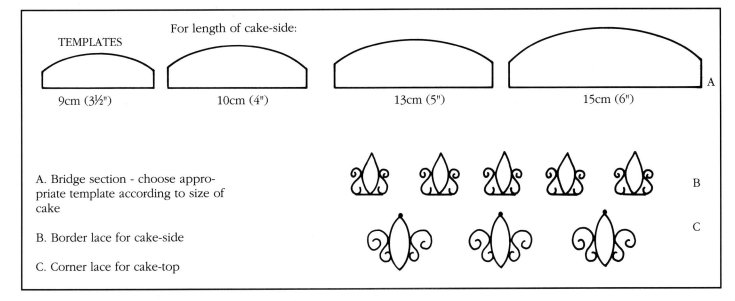

TEMPLATES For length of cake-side:

9cm (3½")   10cm (4")   13cm (5")   15cm (6")   A

A. Bridge section - choose appropriate template according to size of cake

B. Border lace for cake-side

C. Corner lace for cake-top

B

C

PIPING TUBE EMBROIDERY

Embroidery has fascinated people for centuries as almost any combination of colour and stitches is possible. The acorn and strawberry design on p.112 is taken from a traditional l7th century sampler in the Victoria and Albert Museum. Inspiration for embroidery designs can be found almost anywhere: old needlework books will provide a multitude of stitches and designs, and delicate old bone china or fabrics may also fire the imagination. Floral designs and symmetrical, formalised patterns have always been popular and a little experimentation will soon show which of the embroidery stitches adapt best to the medium of icing and to the different cake shapes. Basically, the stitches fall into two groups: the straight stitches suitable for formal patterns on royal iced coated cakes, and the rounded 'soft' stitches which are particularly suitable for more flowing designs on sugarpaste coated cakes or for broderie anglaise work.

Broderie anglaise is extremely effective worked in white or very delicate colours and it can look most attractive on sugarpaste collars for wedding or christening cakes. A suitable embroidery design, or a piece of broderie anglaise fabric, can be used as the basis for a pattern pricked into sugarpaste. A deeper indentation is then made with a knitting needle and, with a No.0 or 00 tube, the hole is filled with icing and then a line carefully piped around in a circle.

Embroidery designs for wedding cakes need to be carefully scaled down for each tier but all designs must be carefully spaced over the area to be filled. A photocopier can be used to quickly enlarge or scale down a design and consideration must be given to the size of cake as some individual stitches may be too small to be practicable. A guide grid can be pricked over the surface of the cake to ensure even and adequate spacing of the design if required.

Before commencing piping, all the colours of icing required for the design should be mixed and placed in small piping bags with a No.0 or 00 tube. A few teaspoons of icing in each colour will be more than sufficient for embroidering a cake. When piping, it is important to continue following the design and to complete each section, changing colours when required and blending the shades if required. A damp paintbrush can be stroked over a join to smooth it out if necessary.

It is easier to work from left to right, unless you are left handed, and care should be taken to ensure that all stitches, such as cross stitch or herringbone, which are crossed by another line, do so in the same direction. A slight variation in pressure may be needed for areas which need special emphasis. The background should be worked first and then the main areas built up to complete the design.

EMBROIDERY STITCHES

1) **Running stitch:** Pipe short even stitches with small gaps between each stitch. (If double running is required, pipe the stitches closer together).

2) **Stem stitch:** Pipe a curved line, tapering off the end. Begin the next stitch halfway along, passing just over the end of the tail.

3) **Chain stitch:** Pipe loops so that the wider, closed end of each loop very slightly overlaps the open end of the previous loop.

4) **Single chain stitch:** Pipe a loop with a longer tail on one side. Pipe a dot at the wider end. (Long or short single chain stitch with a smaller tail can be used for individual petals).

5) **Large french knot:** Pipe a bulb with a tapering tail to the length required.

6) **Small french knot:** Pipe a small bulb with a short tail.

7) **Open cross stitch:** Pipe a row of even sized and spaced oblique lines. Pipe a row of lines in the other direction, crossing at the centre.

8) **Closed cross stitch:** Pipe a row of continuous 'W' stitches and then pipe a row of continuous 'M' stitches over the top, crossing in the middle.

9) **Couching:** Pipe two, or more, continuous horizontal straight lines. At regular intervals, pipe a slightly curved vertical line over the top.

10) **Fern stitch:** Pipe a continuous vertical line down the centre. Pipe oblique lines, equally spaced, above and below the centre line.

11) **Closed buttonhole:** Pipe a series of vertical lines, just touching each other. Pipe a dot at the top of each line.

12) **Open buttonhole:** Beginning at the bottom, pipe a vertical line, finishing off with a downwards tail to one side. Begin the next stitch immediately below the tail end.

13) **Herringbone:** Pipe an oblique line from right to left at the left hand side of the row. Beginning slightly to the left of the top of the first stitch, pipe an oblique left to right line, crossing at the top. Then pipe a right to left line, crossing at top and bottom.

14) **Closed feather stitch:** Pipe open 'U' shapes, beginning each one half-way along the stitch above. (This stitch can be worked as a single line, with stitches to left and right of the first stitch).

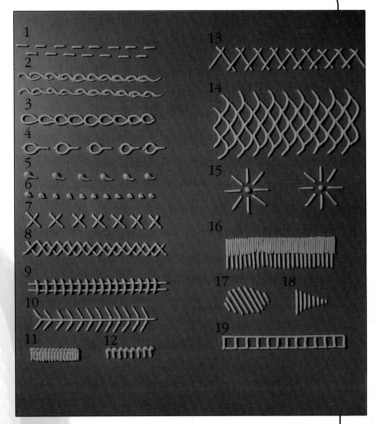

15) **Star stitch:** Pipe a series of straight spokes to form an open wheel. Pipe a dot in the centre.

16) **Long and short stitch:** Pipe a long and then a short straight stitch, just touching. (This stitch can be used for Florentine work).

17) **Satin stitch:** Work a series of straight lines, not quite touching.

18) **Graduated satin stitch:** Satin stitch can be worked to fill any shape.

19) **Holbein stitch:** Work two long straight lines and then work evenly spaced vertical lines just touching top and bottom. (This stitch can be used to fill in an area if required).

ALL MY LOVE

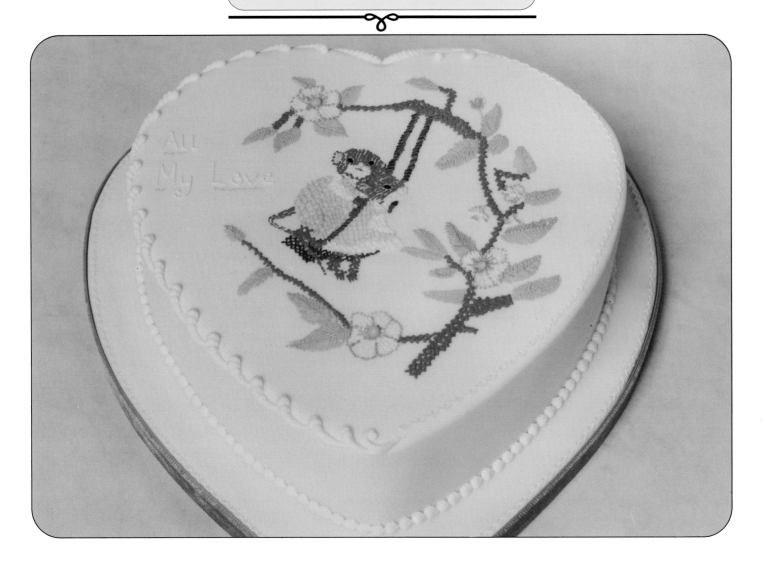

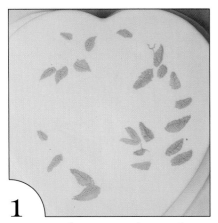

1 Using template as a guide, transfer design to cake-top. Pipe each leaf in satin stitch using royal icing (No.0).

2 Pipe branches using a cross stitch (No.0). Pipe swing ropes in straight stitch.

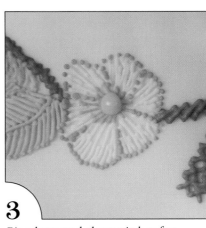

3 Pipe long and short stitches for flower petals (No.0). Outline the flowers with small dots and pipe a centre to each flower (No.0).

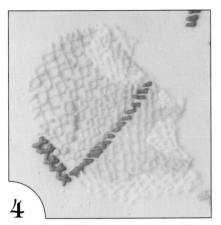

4 Pipe the clothing using cross stitch (No.0).

5 Pipe the heads and tail using straight stitch and then pipe the swing seat and legs in cross stitch (No.0).

6 Decorate the cake and board with piped scrolls (No.42) and decorative lines (No.1). Complete by piping inscription of choice (No.0).

TEMPLATE

1 Score a line on cake-sides for ribbon. Pin prick at intervals 4.5cm (1¾") apart. Pipe shells in royal icing around cake-base (No.2).

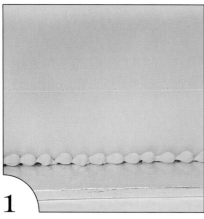

2 Push ribbon into sugarpaste, using flat-headed tool the same width as ribbon. Holding ribbon slack, press it into each pin prick, as shown.

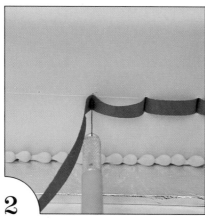

3 To make the sampler, roll out a piece of pastillage. Place fabric on top and re-roll to imprint the weave. Cut out the plaque to required size.

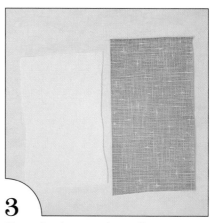

4

Mark the 'hemline' using the edge of a ruler. Mark stitches along the hemline by pressing with a fine point. Leave to dry for 24 hours.

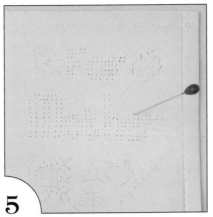

5

Using template as guide, mark out pattern on sampler. Use scratch marks for lines and dots for cross stitches.

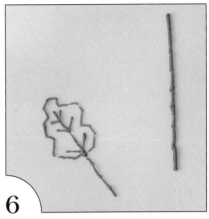

6

Mix royal icing in different colours and fill piping bags with No.0 tubes. Pipe oak leaf lines to simulate double running stitch.

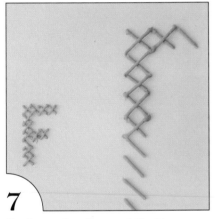

7

Begin to pipe the word 'For' in cross stitch. Pipe diagonals in one direction, then overpipe in opposite direction to complete crosses.

8

Complete the word 'For' and pipe 'Mother' in the same way to complete the first section.

9

To pipe an acorn, pipe horizontal lines in centre to simulate satin stitch. Outline in short lines to simulate double running stitch.

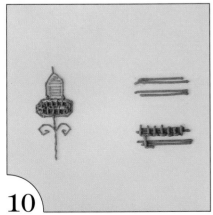

10

Referring to sample, fill in acorn cup with open buttonhole stitch. Outline the cup and pipe stalk and tendrils in double running stitch.

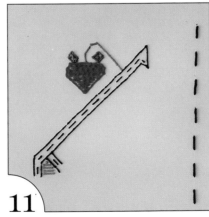

11

Pipe stitches: strawberry- open buttonhole and double running. Centre knot- satin. Diagonals- double running with single running inside.

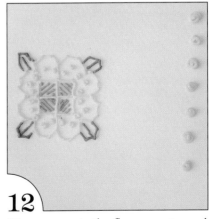

12

Pipe squares in the flower centre and fill in with satin stitch. Continue with double running stitch, adding french knots last.

13

Continue until the middle section of the sampler is completed.

14

Pipe an appropriate date or greeting, as shown.

15

Position the sampler on the cake-top and surround with a border of ribbon. Pipe french knots at each corner (see main picture).

TEMPLATE

TULLE

Tulle is an extremely delicate medium to work in and it produces the most exquisite designs. Only the finest tulle is suitable as a wide mesh would allow the piped royal icing to fall through. Bridal veiling, obtainable at most fabric shops, is ideal. As this is usually only available in white or cream, the tulle can be dyed with a fabric dye for vibrant colours, or soaked in diluted food colouring for a pastel effect. It can also be dusted with petal dust if a very soft effect is required.

There are several ways of using tulle. One way is to cut out the shapes required and then lay them on a flat or curved surface, according to the finished shape required, either on waxed paper or a lightly greased surface. A polystyrene block or tile is ideal as a base as pins can be inserted to keep the tulle taut. The shape is then piped in royal icing. If a complicated pattern is required, the shape can be placed over a template and transferred to a curved surface to dry if necessary. However, it is essential to work quickly as the icing must be wet when moved to prevent cracking. This method can be used for piping the components of three-dimensional models prior to assembly, such as churches, cribs, etc.; or for making figures such as birds, butterflies or the tulle orchid on p.222, which may require supporting with polystyrene or foam until dry. Tulle stiffener (see p.131) may also be used to help pieces keep their shape.

A different method is suitable for clothes, frills, etc. as the tulle is sewn or shaped before piping. Small pieces of foam may be needed to stabilise the item being piped. When working on clothes such as a christening robe or wedding dress, the back should be piped first and allowed to dry before turning the item over and piping the front.

Frills are quickly and easily made following the second method. A strip two and a half times the circumference of the cake is required, the depth depending on the finished design. A scalloped edge can quickly be achieved by folding the frill, concertina fashion, to about 5cm (2") and then cutting one or two scallops in the bottom edge. A running stitch should then be made along the top edge and the frill drawn up to fit the cake, the gathers being evenly distributed along its length. The frill can then be anchored in place with royal icing piped with a No.1 tube, the join being covered by a ribbon. Delicate piping looks extremely attractive on a frill, but the frill can be left plain if desired.

Tulle is also ideal for side decorations or extension work as it can be worked very quickly. The individual pieces should be cut out using a template and carefully attached to the cake with pins before piping a scalloped line over the join. The line should touch both the cake and the tulle. Once the join is dry, the tulle can be piped in an appropriate all-over design to form a decorative border around the cake. When thoroughly dry, the pins should be removed, care being taken not to leave any in the cake.

1

Cover a cake and board in sugarpaste (see p.22). Fix ribbon around cake-base. Using royal icing, pipe shells around cake board edge (No.2).

2

Using template A as guide, cover tracing with waxed paper then pin to a board together with tulle cut to size, as shown.

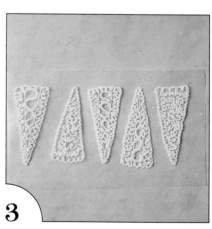

3

Pipe the filigree designs shown, using royal icing (No.1). 6 sets required. Leave to dry for 24 hours.

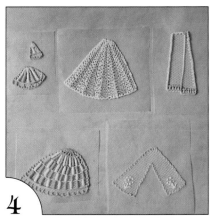

4

Repeat steps 2-3, using templates B-G as guide. 1 of each shape required.

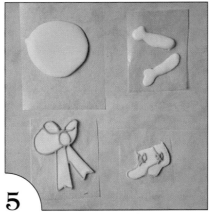

5

Outline and flood-in on waxed paper shapes shown, using templates H-K as guide. Leave to dry for 24 hours.

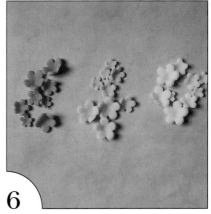

6

Make a variety of sugarpaste blossoms in three sizes and colours. Leave to dry for 24 hours.

7

Fix together the A shaped filigree pieces, to form 6 decorative fans. Leave to dry for 2 hours.

8

Fix a fan into each cake-side curve, as shown.

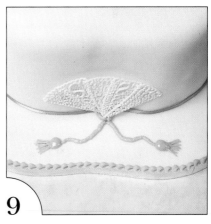

9

Pipe cord and tassels to each fan (No.1).

10

Fix blossoms to cake-top edge and pipe a centre in each (No.1).

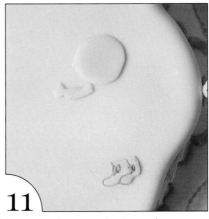

11

Position the runout pieces shown onto the cake-top.

12

Position then fix the pieces as shown, to form the girl.

13 Carefully fix the further parts shown.

14 Carefully fix the remaining pieces to complete the girl.

15 Fix blossoms to the cake-top to form the floral spray shape shown. Pipe inscription of choice (No.1).

TEMPLATES

TRUDY

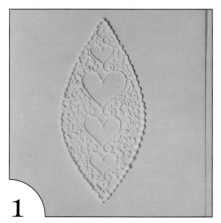

1 Fix the template to a board and cover in waxed paper. Pin the tulle over the template. Pipe design onto tulle using royal icing (No.1).

2 Immediately lift the waxed paper and tulle and lay over a curved surface 7.5cm (3") in diameter. Leave to dry for 24 hours. 6 required.

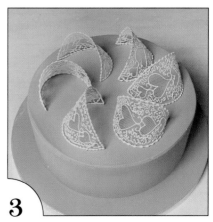

3 Fix the shapes to the cake-top in the position shown.

4 Pipe lines of royal icing around cake-top (No.2). Pipe a line beside the No.2 line and then overpipe the No.2 line (No.1).

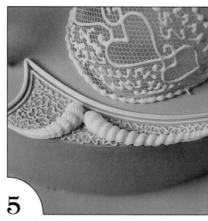

5 Pipe filigree in the areas shown on the cake-top (No.0). Pipe 'S' and 'C' scrolls (No.42), as shown.

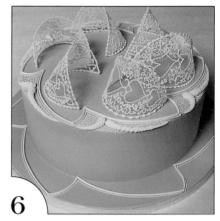

6 Repeat step 4 onto the cake board.

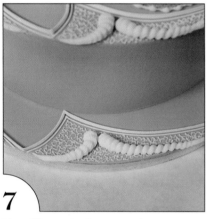

7 Pipe filigree in the areas shown on the cake board (No.0). Pipe 'S' and 'C' scrolls (No.42), as shown.

8 Pipe graduated bulbs around the cake-base (No.3).

9 Pipe heart and flower motifs, as shown (No.1). Fix ribbon around cake-side, and a horseshoe at the cake-base.

TEMPLATES

1

Tulle stiffener: Dissolve 85g (3oz) icing sugar in 145g (5oz) water. Bring to boil and simmer for 10 minutes. Cool and bottle. Store in refrigerator.

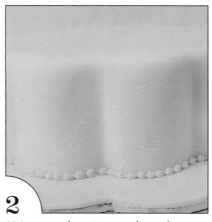

2

Using template A, scratch mark outline for border pattern onto cake-side. Pipe shells in royal icing around the cake-base (No.5).

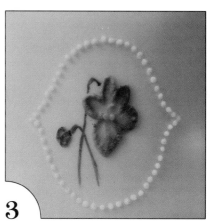

3

Using template B, scratch mark the violets where shown. Brush embroider flowers and paint stems and calyx. Pipe dots, as shown (No.1).

4

Using templates C and D, draw the designs inside the egg moulds. Smear white lard over each mould.

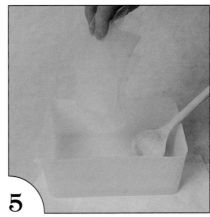

5

Dip cotton tulle into the prepared stiffener. Drain off liquid and remove surplus using kitchen paper.

6

Lay the tulle smoothly over moulds. Twist the spare tulle underneath and fix with a tight elastic band.

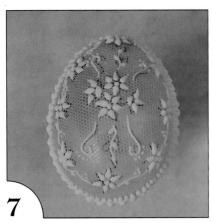

7

Whilst the tulle is still damp, pipe the flowers (No.2) and then lines, leaves and dots (No.1). Pipe a border of tear-drops (No.1).

8

Pipe shallow shells immediately below the tear-drops (No.42). Repeat for second half of the egg mould. Leave to dry for 24 hours.

9

Cut spare tulle level with the edge of the mould using a pair of sharp scissors.

10

Heat oven on lowest setting. Place mould in oven for 1 minute to melt lard. Ease off piped tulle from moulds using a sharp pointed knife.

11

Stand bottom half on a non-stick surface. Pipe a line the shape of the flat area (No.1) and flood-in with royal icing. Leave to dry 12 hours.

12

When the flooding is dry, place an easter egg inside the tulle and fix with royal icing.

13

Fix the halves together at centre back, using royal icing. Support with card (not cotton wool or foam) and leave to dry for 4 hours.

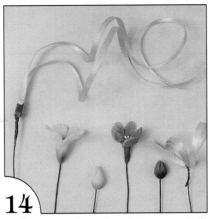

14

Make approximately 10 violets and 6 buds, 10 primroses and 6 buds. Using narrow ribbon, make 24 finger loops and 2 long double tails.

15

Tape up and shape 2 small sprays of prepared flowers and ribbon loops. Pipe inscription of choice (No.0) and fix egg and sprays to cake-top.

TEMPLATES

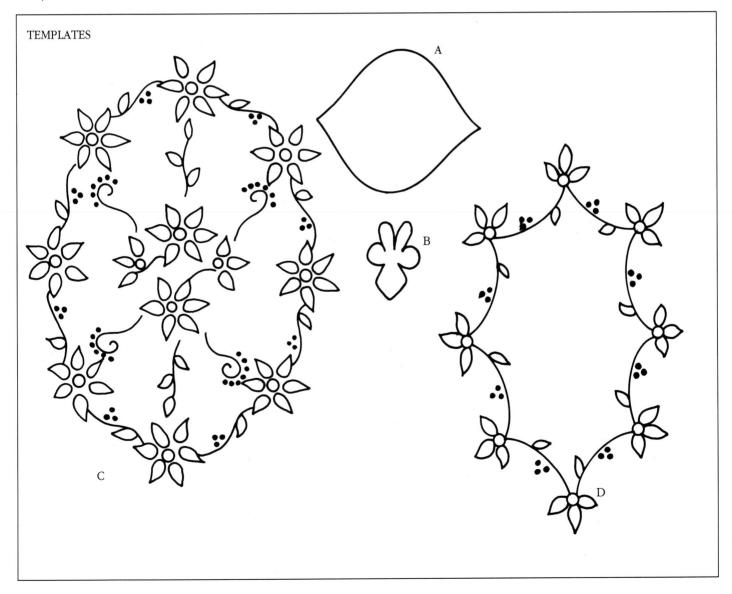

Cake-top decorations can be as simple or as elaborate as the occasion requires - or as the level of skill of the decorator will allow. Striking decorations do not necessarily require a high level of expertise. A simple sugarpaste plaque can, for example, look stunning on a carefully designed and imaginatively coloured cake, and the ingenious Christmas Candles cake on p.145 is extremely easy to create, requiring very little skill and lending itself to an adaptation of colour for other occasions. A simple change to pink or blue trimming, for instance, would make it suitable for a birthday celebration, and a gold or silver 'lining' could create a unique anniversary cake.

With care, skill and flair, however, elaborate decorations can be created to add an individual touch to any celebration cake. Once the basic techniques have been mastered, the designs can be adapted as appropriate. The flower decoration on p.137 could, for instance, be coloured to harmonise with any colour scheme or could replicate almost any flower, and the limousine on p.142 could be adapted to the wedding car, or to any classic car. It would be ideal for a wedding anniversary cake on which the original wedding car was reproduced, or a birthday cake for the proud owner of a veteran car.

The filigree ball on p.135 utilises a very simple technique, that of piping on a balloon, which could be adapted to combine with other runout figures or sugarpaste models to suit any occasion.

When designing cake-tops, it is important to bear in mind not only the occasion but also the overall shape and the effect required. The size and shape of the top and the cake must blend to create a harmonious whole. If the top decoration is too large, then the cake will look top heavy, and too small a decoration will lack impact. Similarly, an inappropriate colour will detract from the overall effect of the cake, whilst imaginative use of colour will enhance its appeal.

SWAN LAKE

1

Blow up a balloon and clip the opening to prevent air escaping. Grease the outside of the balloon lightly with white fat.

2

Fix the balloon in a secure position and begin to pipe a design in royal icing on the outside (No.2).

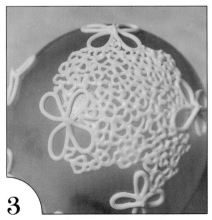

3

Complete the piped filigree design (No.1) and leave in a safe place to dry for 24 hours.

4

Slowly release the air from the balloon and carefully remove it from the iced filigree.

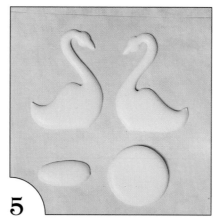

5

Outline and flood-in the swans, bases and plaque onto waxed paper (No.1), using royal icing. Leave to dry for 24 hours.

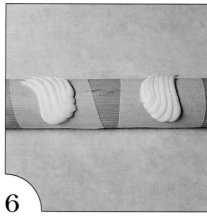

6

Pipe 8 wings onto waxed paper (No.3). Shape the wings by immediately placing them over a rolling pin. Leave to dry for 24 hours.

7

Fix the swans on the bases and paint the eyes and beaks, as shown.

8

Fix the wings to the swans and fix to the central plaque.

9

Add feathers and flowers of choice. Complete the arrangement by placing the filigree ball carefully on top of the plaque.

TEMPLATES

JADE

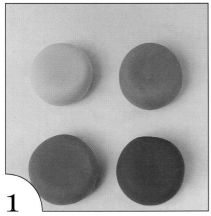

1 Divide 115g (4oz) of flower paste into four and colour each piece differently in colours No's.1-4, as shown.

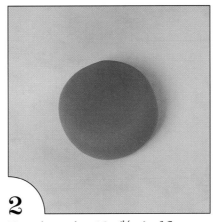

2 Knead together 15g (½oz) of flower paste and 30g (1oz) sugarpaste. Colour the paste to match colour No.3.

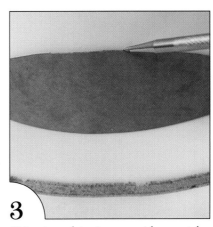

3 Using template A as a guide, scratch a line along the top edge of the template on each curved cake-side, as shown.

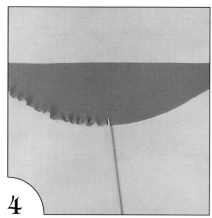

4 Using template B, cut out a side panel from the combined flower paste and sugarpaste. Frill the curved edge.

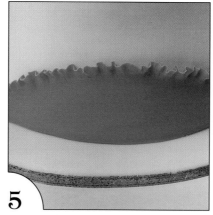

5 Moisten the area on the cake-side below the scratch mark and fix the panel, as shown.

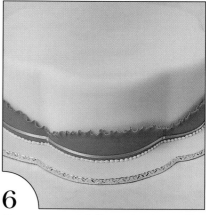

6 Repeat steps 4-5 five more times. Fix a narrow ribbon and then pipe shells of royal icing (No.1) around cake-base.

7 Cut out a 13cm (5") diameter circle from waxed paper and mark a 2.5cm (1") diameter circle in its centre. Cut from edge to centre circle at intervals.

8 Using template C as a guide, cut out a calyx from flower paste in colour No.1. Place the calyx in the centre of the waxed paper.

9 Cut out a petal in colour No.1 using template D. Frill where indicated. Moisten one section of the calyx with egg white and lay petal on top.

10 Cut and fix 6 more petals until the whole calyx is covered. Overlap the petals where necessary.

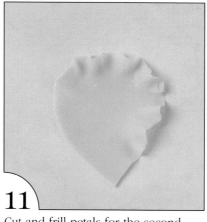

11 Cut and frill petals for the second layer using template E. Cut and frill petals for the third layer using template F.

12 Arrange the second and third layers of petals as in step 10, overlapping and supporting if necessary.

13 Pipe a bead of soft royal icing in the centre of the petals and insert a thick circle of stamens in varying lengths.

14 Make 4 cones using flower paste colour No.2. Thin cones by pressing a modelling tool into centres. Fix to centre and leave to dry 24 hours.

15 Dust the edges of the flower petals, as shown with petal dust.

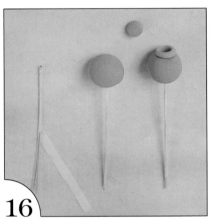

16 Tape together three 9cm (3½") 24 gauge wires. Fix a ball in colour No.3 onto wire for pod. Fix small, flat ball on top. Indent centre to form a ring.

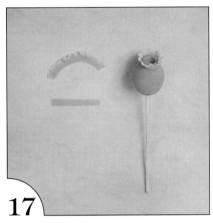

17 To complete the seed pods, roll out a tiny strip of paste and frill. Moisten the outer edge of ring and fix frill, making a neat join.

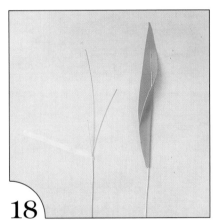

18 Tape a 25, 20 and 15cm (10, 8 and 6") wire together, until 20cm (8") wire is covered. Cut leaf G, colour No.3. Moisten centre, fold leaf over wire.

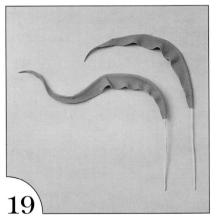

19 Smooth and thin cut edge. Bend wired edge. Twist leaf tip slightly. Repeat using template H, and wires 28, 23 and 18 cm (11, 9 and 7").

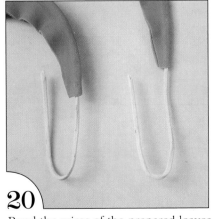

20 Bend the wires of the prepared leaves to form large hooks, as shown.

21 Form ribbon into 1cm (½") loops to be used for decorating the back of the arrangement.

22

Roll out and cut a thick paste leaf, colour No.4, using template I. Insert a hooked 10cm (4"), 24 gauge wire 1cm (½") into leaf.

23

Gently press the leaf onto a veiner or plastic leaf to mark veins. Thin all edges by pressing hard.

24

Carefully remove the leaf from the veiner and support edges to give a natural shape. Leave to dry. Make 2 more leaves using template J.

25

Fix the flower to a large ball of sugarpaste onto the cake-top, in the position shown.

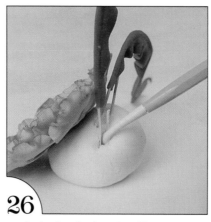

26

Push the hooked ends of leaves into the paste, firming with a modelling tool between and behind the hooks to secure.

27

Push the wires of the seed pods into the paste, behind the leaves and flower.

28

Push the oak leaf wires into the ball of paste, positioning as shown.

29

Begin to push the loops of ribbon into the ball of paste at the back of the arrangement.

30

Cover the remainder of the paste ball with ribbon loops, taking care that they cannot be seen from the front of the arrangement.

JADE continued

TEMPLATES

C

G

H

D

Frill

E

Frill

J

F

Frill

B

A

141

1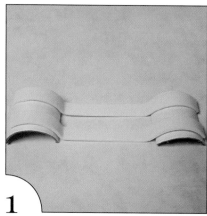

Using templates as guides, cut out pieces from Mexican paste. Shape running boards to form wheel arches. Leave to dry for 24 hours.

2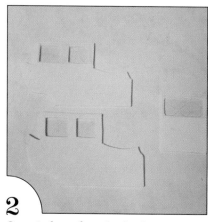

Cut windows from leaf gelatine and fix, with royal icing, over the cut-outs on the side and front car pieces.

3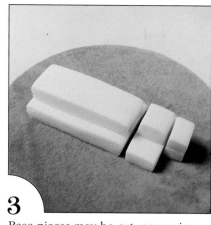

Base pieces may be cut, approximately 1cm (½") thick, from either sugarpaste or Mexican paste. Arrange the pieces on a board, as shown.

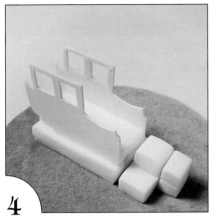

4 Fix the side panels to the base using royal icing.

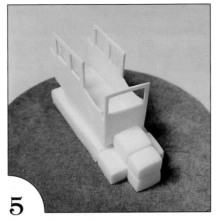

5 Fix the front windscreen panel. Push up and fix the front base panels to secure the windscreen panel.

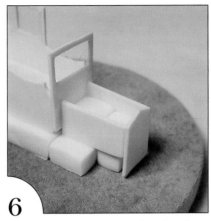

6 Fix the side engine panel and radiator grill, as shown.

7 Fix the bonnet panels, wheels and running boards, as shown.

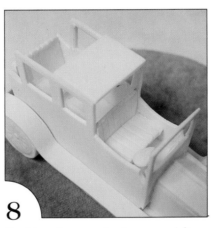

8 Position the seats in the car and fix the roof and steering wheel.

9 Decorate the limousine with piped royal icing lines and then shells (No.0).

10 Paint the piped detail very carefully with gold edible lustre colour. Make and fix lights and lamps, as shown.

11 Make a looped bow from very narrow ribbon and fix to the bonnet.

12 Cut a plaque from sugarpaste and fix to the board. Pipe inscription of choice onto plaque (No.0).

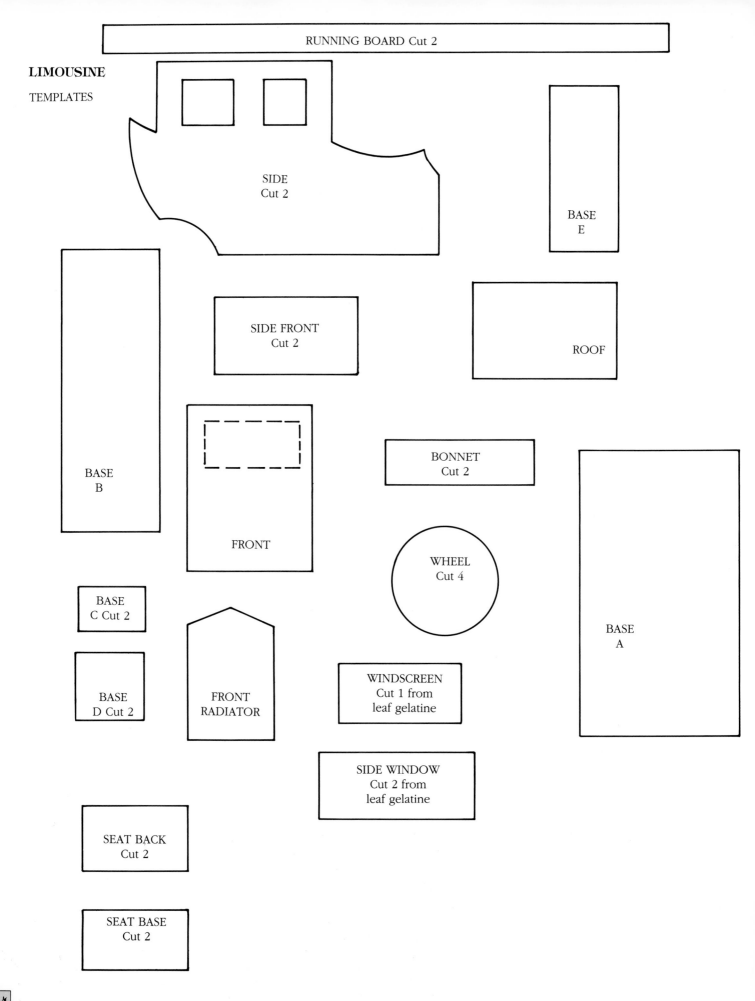

RUNNING BOARD Cut 2

LIMOUSINE

TEMPLATES

SIDE
Cut 2

BASE
E

SIDE FRONT
Cut 2

ROOF

BASE
B

BONNET
Cut 2

FRONT

BASE
C Cut 2

WHEEL
Cut 4

BASE
A

BASE
D Cut 2

FRONT
RADIATOR

WINDSCREEN
Cut 1 from
leaf gelatine

SIDE WINDOW
Cut 2 from
leaf gelatine

SEAT BACK
Cut 2

SEAT BASE
Cut 2

1 Cut and fix sugarpaste to cake-top. Leave to dry for 24 hours. Cut greaseproof same size as cake-top, and another 10cm (4") smaller.

2 Place the small disc of greaseproof in centre of cake-top and moisten remaining area. Cut green sugarpaste to fit cake-top and fix. Smooth.

3 Immediately place the cake on a board and cover both in sugarpaste.

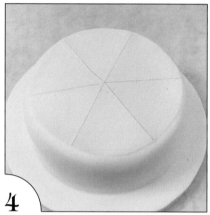

4 Fold the larger disc of greaseproof paper into 6. Using it as a guide, mark the sugarpaste along the fold lines with a knife.

5 Carefully cut along the marks ensuring both layers are cut. Take care not to damage the underneath layer. Fold back the sugarpaste.

6 When all the sections are folded back, carefully remove the protective disc of greaseproof paper.

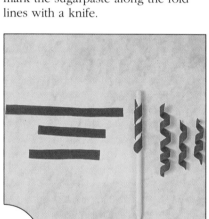

7 Using Mexican paste, cut 3 strips, one longer than the others. Wrap around dowelling to form candles. Leave to dry for 24 hours.

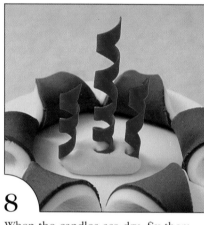

8 When the candles are dry, fix them into a piece of sugarpaste in the centre of the cake-top.

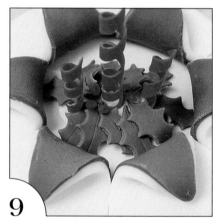

9 Cut holly leaves from sugarpaste and fix to cake-top. Berries can be added if required.

10 Form rolls of red, white and green sugarpaste to fit the circumference of the cake-base. Twist the rolls together, as shown.

11 Moisten the twisted roll and fix to the cake-base.

12 Pipe flames, using royal icing, onto the tips of the candles (No.3).

PIPING GEL

Piping gel is an extremely easy medium to use as it is slow-drying, has excellent keeping properties and its effect can be simple or sophisticated. It has a shiny, transparent finish which can be colourful or subtle according to the colours chosen. It is ideal for use by busy mums who need an instant effect, or by children who will enjoy creating new characters or copying old favourites.

Many suitable designs can be found in books, on birthday or Christmas cards, or on the popular transfers which are available for teenagers and children. Beginners should choose a fairly simple design but anyone with artistic flair and imagination will soon be able to create a masterpiece.

Clear gel is available from most sugarcraft outlets. This can be coloured as required using liquid or paste food colouring. Ready-made colours, in tubes, are also available from major supermarkets. These basic colours can be mixed to form different shades. A little colour at a time should be mixed, remembering that a little really does go a very long way indeed with this medium. Plates, tiles or a marble slab make ideal 'palettes' for mixing. The coloured gel should then be transferred to a small piping bag without a tube, and a different bag will be required for each colour.

Piping gel is suitable for use on royal iced, sugarpaste or buttercream-coated cakes. When working, each colour section of the design should be completely outlined in royal icing or piping chocolate (see p.148) and then piped-in as appropriate with the gel. As the colour is piped in individual sections, there is no need to wait for one section to dry before commencing another.

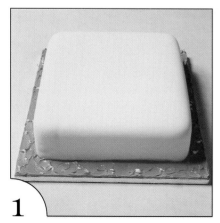

1

Cover a sponge in white sugarpaste (see p.22). Coat the cake board in royal icing and stipple, as shown.

2

Using the templates as a guide transfer designs to the cake-top and sides (see p.33). Pipe the lines with royal icing (No.1), as shown.

3

Colour neutral piping gel with either liquid or paste colourings, or use ready-coloured piping gel to fill in the pirate.

4

Fill in the objects around the cake-side as described in step 3.

5

Pipe a continuous rope line around the cake-base (No.44).

6

Pipe inscription of choice onto the cake-top (No.1).

TEMPLATES

1
Transfer design (see p.33) of choice onto cake-top and outline with royal icing (No.1).

2
Colour neutral piping gel to colours of choice and fill in each section, as shown.

3
Pipe royal icing 'C' scrolls and shells (No.43) and scalloped lines on board (No.2, 1). Pipe inscription of choice (No.1). Fix ribbons.

COCOA PAINTING

Cocoa painting is a most attractive medium, which is used in a similar way to oil paints, in several shades of brown. Painting can either be directly onto the cake or onto a sugarpaste or marzipan plaque, in which case it can be removed and kept as a memento of the occasion.

Inspiration for designs can be found in sepia or black and white photographs, in the slate plaques on which animals are often featured, or in cards which have been printed in several shades of one colour. Proficient artists may well enjoy creating their own design to match the particular interests of the recipient.

As brown tones well with cream, yellow or apricot shades, sugarpaste for a plaque can be lightly coloured before rolling out. The final background colour chosen depends on the subject matter. After tracing the design onto greaseproof paper, use a brown lip-liner pencil to go over the lines on the reverse side of the paper. The design should then be sketched or traced with minimal detail onto the cake or plaque (see p.152). If too many lines are used, they may well show through light painted tones and affect the finished appearance.

Begin by painting the background areas in the lightest shade and then progress to the medium tone and to the darker shade. Finally, fill in the eyes, etc., and any shadows with the very dark mix. Once the plaque is dry, a scalpel can be used to scratch or scrape away some of the colour to form highlights and textures such as fur or grass.

Cocoa Solution

To prepare the cocoa, place a teaspoon of white vegetable fat, coconut oil or cocoa butter (available from health stores) into each of four small containers. The containers should be heat-proof as they are then placed in a pan of hot water. Begin by adding a little cocoa to the first container to produce a very light shade, then gradually add a little more to the other containers to make darker shades. Finally, in the last container make a dark brown shade which is used for filling in features and shadows. The water may need to be reheated from time to time while painting if the mixtures become too stiff. The containers can be covered with a cloth and left overnight if necessary, simply reheating the water the next day.

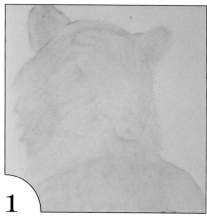

1 Using template as guide, transfer the design to a dry sugarpaste plaque. Using a pale solution of cocoa mixture (see p.151), paint the base coat.

2 Using increasingly darker solutions, paint further detail on the tiger's head.

3 Using the darkest solution, paint in the final detail, as shown.

4 Fix plaque to cake-top. Make and fix two more plaques. Pipe inscription (No.1). Pipe royal icing shells around plaque-edge (No.2).

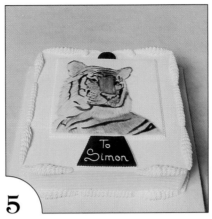

5 Pipe spiral shells at each corner (No.7). Pipe a rope between each cake-side centre (No.7).

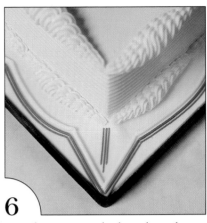

6 Pipe lines onto cake board, as shown (No's.3, 2 and 1).

TEMPLATE

RUSTY

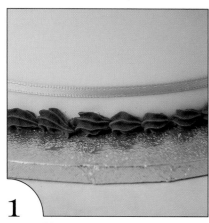

1 Fix a ribbon around the cake-side and pipe shells of royal icing around the cake-base, as shown (No.7).

2 Trace border design and transfer to cake-side. Paint design with cocoa solution (see p.151). Brush with moistened white petal powder for snow.

3 Make a tiny sugarpaste cone and flatten underside. Shape stalk from thick end and snip with scissors. Fix 2 to each branch. Brush with 'snow'.

4
Trace outline of squirrel template and transfer to cake-top. Paint background with light solution, omitting area of snow on branch.

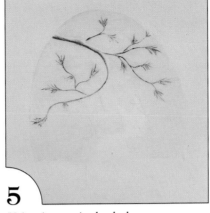

5
Using increasingly darker cocoa solutions, paint in the branches and leaves with a fine paintbrush.

6
Referring to the main photograph, begin to paint the squirrel in a light colour, omitting the white areas. Use short, fine strokes to represent fur.

7
Again using short, fine brush strokes, paint over the first layer to increase the depth of colour, as required.

8
Paint in detail with the darkest tone. Ensure the squirrel has an even spread of tones.

9
Paint in the grass, footprints and other detail in the foreground.

10
To complete the fur effect, scratch off some of the colour using a sharp point. In the same way, make contrasts, such as light in the eye.

11
Scrape away any unwanted cocoa from the frame area. Outline and flood-in frame onto the cake-top using softened royal icing (No.0).

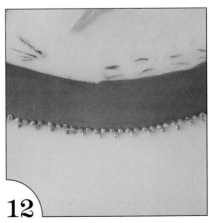

12
Decorate the outside edge of the frame by piping with royal icing, as shown (No.0). 'Gild' with lustre colour.

TEMPLATES

BAS-RELIEF

Bas-relief is a two-dimensional sculpting technique which dates back at least as far as ancient Egypt, and which can be adapted for cake decoration with striking results. In bas-relief, the figure projects to no more than half its true depth above the background, an illusion of height and depth being created by depressing, raising or layering appropriate areas of the design. It is usually worked in sugarpaste on a ready-prepared plaque or directly onto the top, or sides, of a sugarpaste-coated cake which has been allowed to dry for at least 24 hours. Flowerpaste can be used for delicate areas which need to dry to shape, such as the dragon's wing feathers, and Mexican paste for areas that require more strength, as in the frills on the Pierrot.

This technique offers great scope for imaginative design and use of colour, and almost any subject is appropriate. Flowers or animals are universal favourites but mythological beasts such as the Gurt Vurm make a dramatic impact. The effect can be heightened by the imaginative use of colour combined with techniques such as painting or brush embroidering the background. A simple yet effective 'marble' plaque can be created by repeatedly rolling together two different shades of sugarpaste. If the background is to be painted or piped, this should be completed, and allowed to dry, before commencing work on the relief itself.

When a suitable design has been selected, it should be traced and carefully transferred to the cake or plaque (see p.33) and a template prepared for the relief section if necessary.

To prepare sugarpaste for bas-relief work, knead ¼ teaspoon of gum tragacanth into 60g (2oz) of sugarpaste, cover and leave for 2 hours. The sugarpaste should be rolled out to an appropriate thickness (usually 5mm (¼")), having been coloured first if required, and the relief cut out with a sharp knife. The cut-out shape should be lightly moistened and carefully positioned within the marked outline on the cake or plaque. The cut edges should be lightly smoothed with a fingertip or ball-shaped modelling tool.

When modelling bas-relief, it is important to start with the areas which will be lower than, or behind, other areas. A ball-shaped modelling tool should be used to depress or raise these areas, and raised parts may require a small piece of paste tucking underneath. Clothes, or a layered design such as the dragon, should be built up in stages and a modelling tool used to create folds or movement in clothes, etc. where appropriate. Painting should be carried out with a fine paintbrush and edible liquid or paste food colouring or confectioners' dusting powder, care being taken not to make the paste too wet. Colour should be tested on a spare, dry piece of sugarpaste first. Begin by painting the delicate, light areas and then the darker areas can be added gradually. Finishing touches may be added by piping in decoration such as hair, buttons, stamens or other fine detail.

PUPPY LOVE

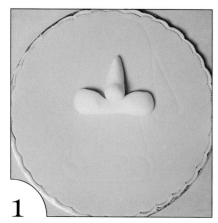

1

Transfer design to plaque (see p.33). Make and fix nose and cheeks from sugarpaste.

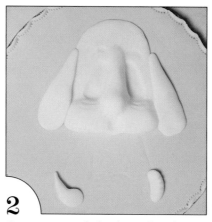

2

Cover nose and cheeks with a thin layer of sugarpaste shaped for head. Make and fix ears, tail and front paw. Indent eye sockets and creases.

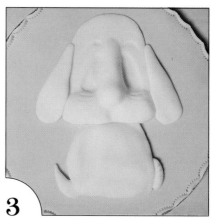

3

Cut body from sugarpaste and fix to plaque, as shown. Smooth and taper all outer edges. Indent body to take paw and leg.

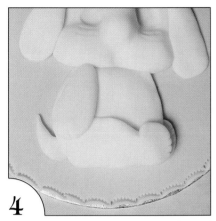

4

Fix paw and leg to puppy's body and carefully smooth all surfaces. Mark all paws with a craft knife.

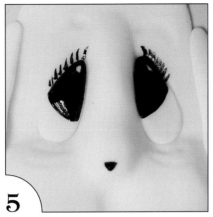

5

Fill the eye sockets with large teardrops of white sugarpaste and paint half with black food colouring. Paint lashes and nose, as shown.

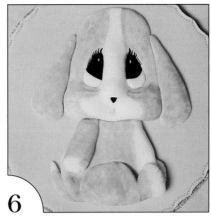

6

Colour Puppy Love, creating a stippled effect by dabbing with a sponge. Complete with decoration of choice.

TEMPLATE

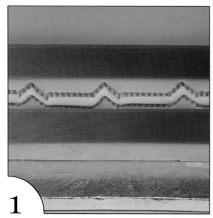

1

Fix 1cm (½") ribbon bands 1cm (½") apart around the cake-side. Using straight and V-shape crimpers alternately, crimp between the ribbon.

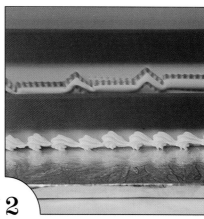

2

Pipe a small scroll border in royal icing around the cake-base, beneath the lower ribbon band (No.5). Leave to dry for 24 hours.

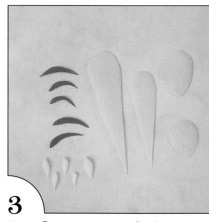

3

From flower paste, cut feathers using templates A-D. Thin edges and shape (5 of each required). Form 5 teeth and claws. Leave to dry.

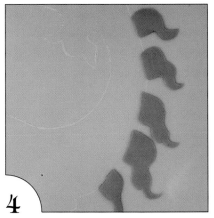

4

Trace template E and position on cake-top. Scratch mark outline. Cut chest fringes from sugarpaste using templates F-J, moisten and fix.

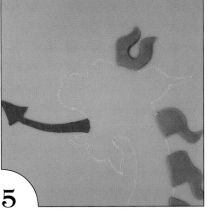

5

Cut out sugarpaste horns using template K and smooth edges. Using template L, cut tongue. Moisten and fix pieces into position.

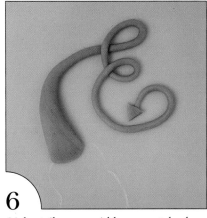

6

Make tail same width as scratched outline. Fix wide end in position and form extension into initial letter of name. Add triangle to tip.

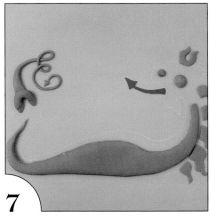

7

Cut tail curl with template M. Cut body padding with template N from 6mm (¼") sugarpaste, tapering ends. Make nose and cheek padding. Fix.

8

Roll out sugarpaste to 6mm (¼") thick. Cut out allowing 3mm (⅛") extra each side of body and fill body following scratch line. Indent face.

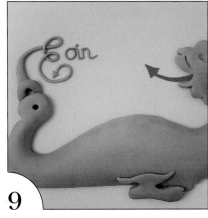

9

Cut out foot using template 0. Smooth and round edges, moisten and fix. Pipe remainder of name in royal icing (No.2).

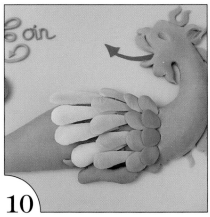

10

Dust prepared wing feathers with confectioners' dusting powder and push into position, as shown.

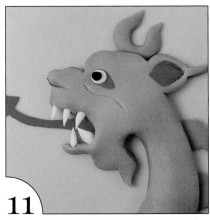

11

Line ear, nostril and eye socket with sugarpaste. Pipe eye (No.1) and fix teeth in position. Pipe centre to eye (No.1). Indent ear.

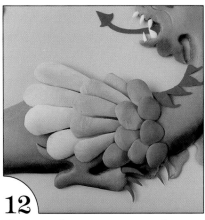

12

Cut mane from sugarpaste, using template P, and fix. Dust under chest, body and darken beard. Fix in claws. Make and fix a numeral.

TEMPLATES

PIERROT

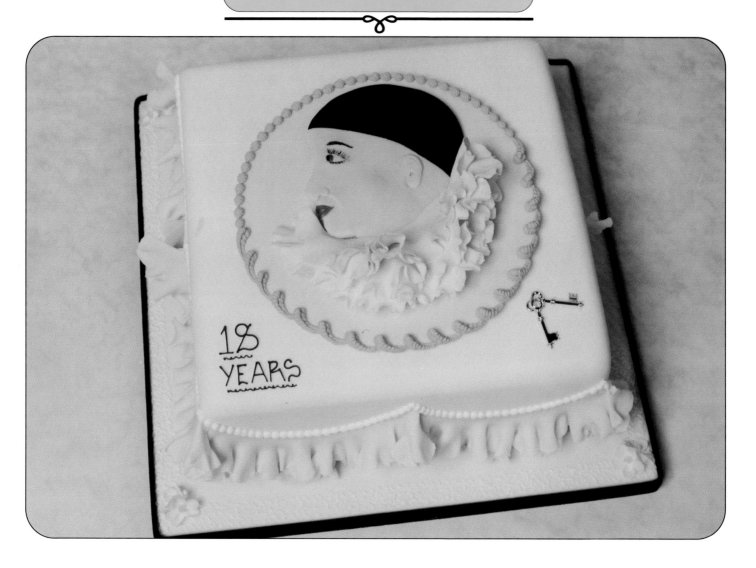

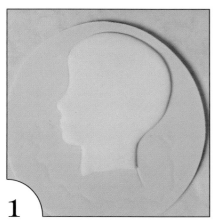

1 Mark position of frills on a sugarpaste plaque. Using the template as a guide, cut out the profile from sugarpaste and fix to a dry plaque.

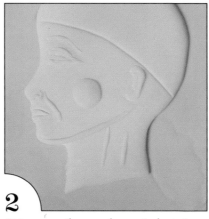

2 Using a scriber, make an indentation for skull cap. Fix sugarpaste shapes to form raised features and facial detail, as shown.

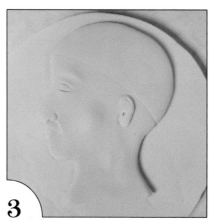

3 Using Mexican paste, cut out profile slightly larger than template. Fix over prepared surface, smoothing carefully to emphasise features.

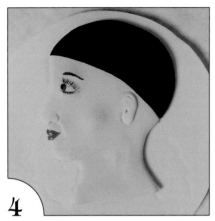

4 Paint in the skull cap and facial details using edible food colourings.

5 Cut and make 3 frills from Mexican paste and fix around the neck, as shown.

6 Pipe royal icing scrolls around plaque edge and fix to cake-top, as shown (No.42). Decorate cake as required.

TEMPLATE

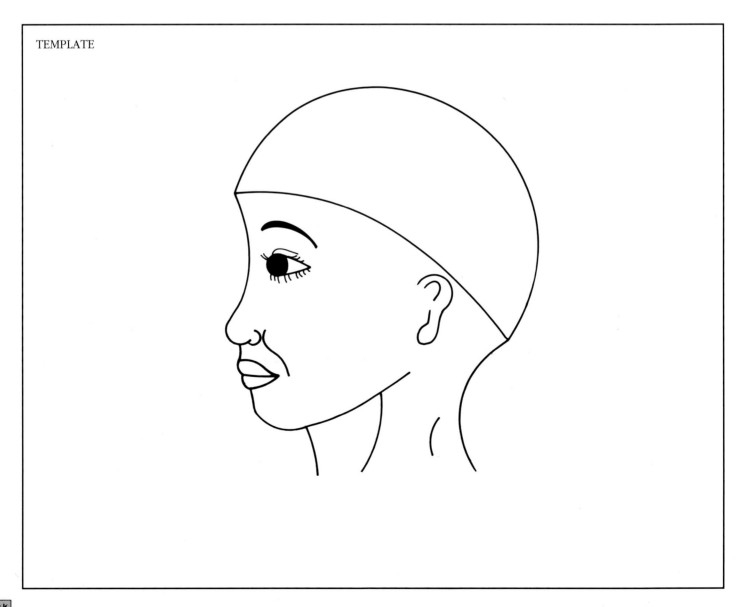

1 Cut out the angel, using template A as a guide, and place on the cake-top. Mark the outline of the angel by scratching round the template.

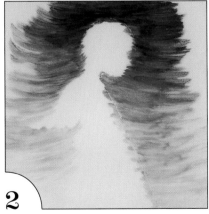

2 Colour-wash the background with diluted paste colour, taking care not to paint over the edges of the wing. Avoid using excessive liquid.

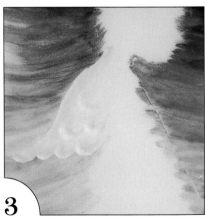

3 Brush embroider (see p.186) the wing using royal icing (No.1).

4

Using template, cut out a sugarpaste body (omitting wing) 6mm (¼") thick and fix to cake-top. Fix a small ball under face to pad cheek.

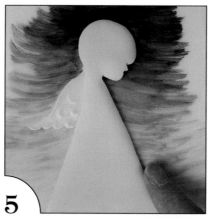

5

Using a finger, or modelling tool, smooth all the edges to curve and neaten.

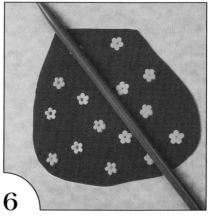

6

Roll out flower paste thinly. Cut out blossoms and lay at random on the rolled out paste. Roll again before cutting out dress using template B.

7

Moisten body, at sides and neck. Position dress over body. Smooth edges and arrange fullness. Colour cheek and paint in eye and lips.

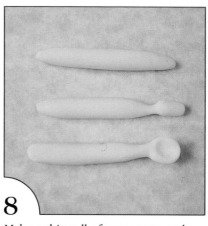

8

Make a thin roll of sugarpaste and shape at one end for the wrist. Press a modelling tool into the hand section to shape the palm, as shown.

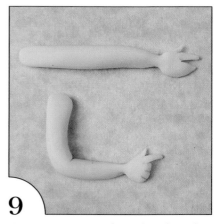

9

Cut 'V' sections to form thumb and forefinger. Turn remainder under and indent for other fingers. Bend arm to shape. Leave to dry 6 hours.

10

Cut out flower paste sleeve template C. Moisten underside of upper arm edge and top. Lay over arm. Fix edges. Curl under lower edge and fix.

11

Brush some royal icing over head to colour the scalp and overpipe with strands of royal icing to create hair (No.0). Decorate sleeve edge.

12

Using template D, pipe halo of snowflakes, leaves and grasses onto waxed paper (No.0). Leave to dry 4 hours. Decorate cake as required.

TEMPLATES

A

B

C

D

ROYAL ICED CAKES

Royal icing is the traditional medium for celebration cakes and its beautiful smooth finish is perfect for formal piped designs such as wedding cakes. To produce a good finish, it is essential that great care be taken when making the icing and coating the cake as the slightest lump will mar the smoothness. For this reason, all items used in preparation, coating and decorating should be scrupulously clean.

Royal icing is a form of meringue and, therefore, must be well beaten. Failure to do so can result in a heavy icing which is difficult to handle and may set very hard. On the other hand, over-beating royal icing, for example using a high speed beater, injects too much air into the mixture and causes it to become fluffy. Correctly prepared royal icing has a clean, white colour and is slightly glossy and light in texture. If the icing sugar is added too quickly, the icing will be heavy and grainy in appearance. Under-mixed icing will have a slightly creamy look and should be beaten further. Poorly made icing will set to a chalky appearance and will be difficult to work.

The icing should be made with fresh egg white or albumen solution and care should be taken that no yolk is included. A table for soft cutting royal icing will be found on p.18. The consistency of royal icing varies with the type of work involved and some icing can be made 24 hours in advance, whereas other techniques require freshly made icing. Bowls of icing should be covered with a clean damp cloth to prevent drying out, or should be stored in a closed container in a refrigerator. Icing which has been removed from a refrigerator must be allowed to reach room temperature before working. If shells or other shapes are to be piped, then the consistency needs to be sufficiently stiff to hold its shape with well defined edges and peaks. For writing, or piping long lines, the icing needs to be slightly softer as otherwise it will break. Flood-in icing requires a much softer, runny consist-

ency and an easy test is to thin down a small quantity of royal icing and then draw a sharp knife across the top. The line should close up on a count of 7 in warm weather and 10 in cold conditions. Icing for runout and No.1 work should not have glycerin added and should stand overnight to allow any bubbles to rise to the surface.

A very small amount of blue colour can be incorporated into the icing to improve the whiteness but blue should never be added to icing which is to be coloured further as it will adversely affect the colour. The easiest way to colour icing is to add a few drops of liquid food colouring on the end of a cocktail stick or skewer. Sufficient icing to complete the work should always be mixed at one time as it is almost impossible to match the colour exactly at a later date.

Icing for coating should be made 24 hours in advance and stirred immediately before use to disperse any bubbles. The consistency should form soft peaks and a drop of water can be added if the icing is too stiff to spread easily. When storing the icing, it should be covered with food-approved polythene or kept in an airtight container in a refrigerator. When working with royal icing, a small amount should be placed in a separate bowl (which can be covered with a damp cloth if required) and the remainder sealed in the main container. The icing in the separate bowl should be kept well scraped down to prevent it drying out, but if bits do form they will not contaminate the main batch.

Getting as good a shape as possible at the almond paste or marzipan stage will make coating the cake easier as it enables a smooth layer of icing to be laid down. The cake should be prepared by either levelling the top of a dome-shaped cake, or removing the outer edges of a sunken cake. Any imperfections can be filled in with almond paste, and any burnt fruit should be removed from the surface of the cake. The cake should be placed in the centre of the board, without fixing it in any way. When rolling out almond paste, use icing or caster sugar for dusting, **never** use cornflour as this causes fermentation. When fixing the almond paste to the cake, always use boiling apricot pureé as this prevents mould or fermentation. The layer of almond paste must be sufficiently thick to prevent the cake from discolouring the icing. Always ensure that the almond paste covered cake has a level top and vertical sides as this will make coating easier. When the covering is complete, the cake should be left to stand in a warm room (18°C/65°F) for three to four days. Do not store a covered cake in a sealed plastic container.

Helpful Hints For Coating
Always coat a cake with royal icing that has been left standing for 24 hours, and stir the icing immediately before use.

As the cake will be difficult to move once coated, ensure that it is correctly positioned on the board prior to commencing coating. Three layers are required for perfect coating (see p.26) and each layer must be allowed to dry thoroughly. Trim each layer, where necessary, with a sharp knife before applying the next. Each layer should be applied as quickly as possible. Do not dip the palette knife or ruler in water when applying royal icing.

Coloured icing will dry to a patchy finish if the coating is uneven. When coating, put a quantity of royal icing on top of the cake and 'paddle' it backwards and forwards with a palette knife, rotating the turntable at the same time so that any bubbles come to the surface and burst.

Spread the icing with the knife or scraper held at a 45° angle, and return any surplus icing to the bowl.

Tools For Coating
A stiff, stainless steel palette knife is ideal for spreading royal icing, and a stainless steel ruler can be used for flattening and levelling the top surface. Side scrapers which are not too flexible should be selected as this will produce a smooth finish. Plastic or stainless steel scrapers are best. When using a side scraper, the fingers should be spread across the width of the scraper to ensure even pressure when rotating the turntable. This will avoid dense slopes or grooves around the cake-side. Any scratches in the ruler or scraper should be removed by rubbing with emery cloth.

The turntable is the most important tool in aiding coating with royal icing. As with all tools that have moving parts, it does need lubricating with either food-approved oil or grease to make the top rotate with a smooth motion. If a turntable is not available, an upturned plate can be used to improvise.

Non-ferrous tools should always be used for royal icing.

Storage
After the cake has been decorated, it should be stored in a cardboard box, which enables the cake to 'breath' and air to circulate to keep it dry.

Decorating Cakes Coated With Royal Icing
The introductory section to Royal Icing Designs on p.72 contains advice and information on piping and decorating with royal icing and should be referred to before commencing work. Advice on sizing, timing and tiering a cake will be found in the introductory section to Wedding Cakes on p.224.

CLARISSA

1 Coat a cake and fix on a double board in the position shown.

2 Using flowers of choice, make and fix an appropriate spray to the cake-top.

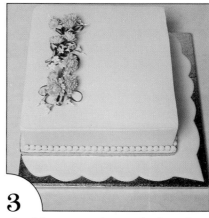

3 Fix ribbon around top cake board. Pipe shells of royal icing around cake-base (No.43). Outline and flood-in cake board design with royal icing (No.2).

4

Pipe inscription of choice on the cake-top (No.1).

5

Decorate the inscription (No.0) and fix sugar birds (see p.246), as shown.

6

Pipe a series of 'S' and 'C' scrolls around the cake-top edge (No.43).

7

Pipe the remaining cake-top edge with shells and scrolls in royal icing (No.43).

8

Overpipe the scrolls, as shown (No.2).

9

Pipe a 'C' line on each shell (No.2), then overpipe No.2 lines (No.1).

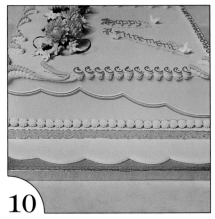

10

Pipe a series of scalloped lines around the cake-sides using various shades of royal icing (No's.2, 1 and 0).

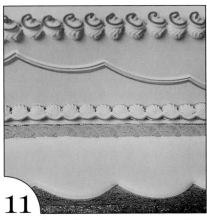

11

Pipe a line of royal icing over each cake-base shell (No.2), then overpipe the No.2 line (No.1).

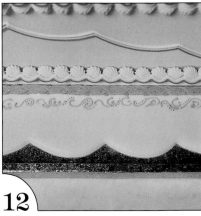

12

Decorate the cake board with a series of scrolls and dots in royal icing (No.0). Fix a spray to the cake board.

1

Using sugar flowers of choice, foliage and ribbon loops, make up a decorative floral wreath, as shown.

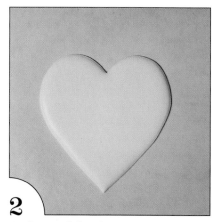

2

Outline and flood-in, on waxed paper (see p.35), a heart-shaped runout (No.1). Leave to dry for 24 hours.

3

Decorate the heart, as shown, and pipe inscription of choice (No.1 and 0).

4 Pipe a line of royal icing around the cake-base (No.44).

5 Divide the cake-top into 48 sections and pipe an 'S' scroll in each section (No.42).

6 Pipe another 48 'S' scrolls around the cake-base, keeping them in line with those above (No.42).

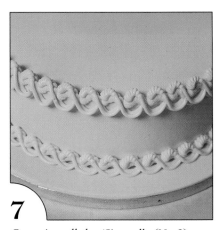

7 Overpipe all the 'S' scrolls (No.3).

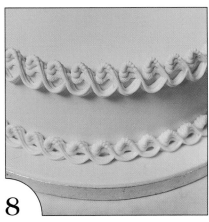

8 Overpipe each scroll (No.2).

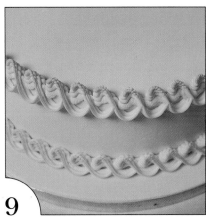

9 Overpipe each scroll (No.1).

10 Pipe a scalloped rope beside each scroll on the cake-top, cake-side and board, as shown (No.2).

11 Place the wreath of sugar flowers on the cake-top and fix the heart in the centre.

12 Decorate the cake-base with small sprays of sugar flowers, foliage and ribbon loops, as shown.

SELINA

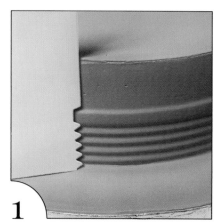

1

Coat a cake with royal icing. Use a patterned scraper, as shown, on the final coat. Leave to dry for 24 hours.

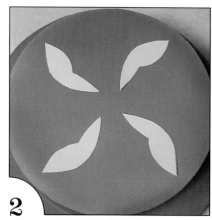

2

Trace and cut out the templates. Place on the cake-top and mark the positions.

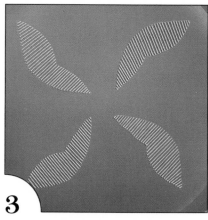

3

Pipe straight lines of royal icing within the marked shapes (No.0).

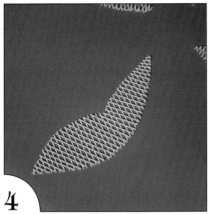

4
Pipe lines across the first lines to form lattice (No.0).

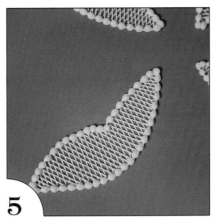

5
Pipe shells around the edge of each shape (No.1).

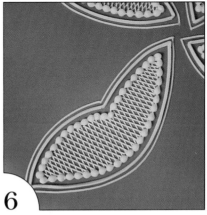

6
Pipe a line around each shape (No.2). Pipe a line beside the No.2 line (No.1), then overpipe the No.2 line (No.1).

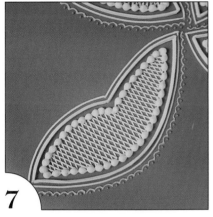

7
Pipe a scalloped line along the long edge of each shape (No.0). Pipe a dot inside each scallop, as shown (No.0).

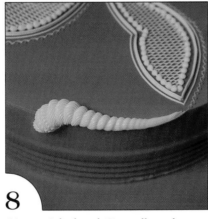

8
Pipe a right hand 'S' scroll on the edge of the cake-top, in the position shown (No.43).

9
Pipe a left hand 'S' scroll (No.43). Repeat three more times to cover the whole of the cake-top edge, as shown.

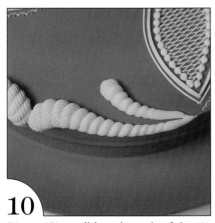

10
Pipe a 'C' scroll beside each of the 'S' scrolls, as shown (No.43).

11
Picture shows completed cake-top with all 'S' and 'C' scrolls.

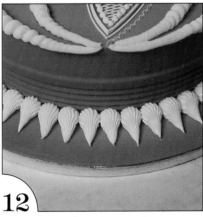

12
Pipe shells of royal icing, facing outwards, round the cake-base, as shown (No.43).

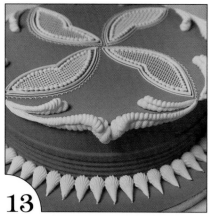

13 Overpipe all the scrolls (No.3).

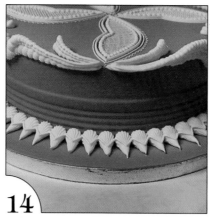

14 Overpipe the scrolls (No.2). Pipe a zigzag design over the shells, as shown (No.2).

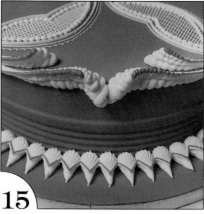

15 Overpipe the scrolls and zigzag design (No.1).

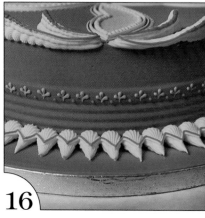

16 Pipe a floral pattern along the wide band made by the patterned scraper on the cake-side (No.0).

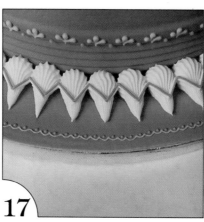

17 Pipe a scalloped line around the cake board (No.0). Pipe a dot inside each scallop, as shown (No.0).

18 Pipe shells around the cake board edge (No.2) and then pipe a line over each shell (No.1).

TEMPLATES

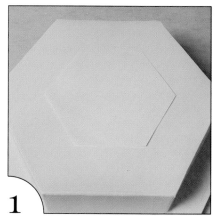

1 Cut out an appropriate template and place on the cake-top, as shown.

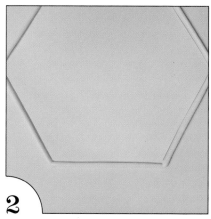

2 Pipe around the edge of the template in royal icing (No.4). Carefully remove the template.

3 Pipe a line each side of the No.4 line (No.3), then overpipe the No.4 line (No.3).

4
Pipe a line around the cake-base (No.44).

5
Pipe a line beside the inside and outside lines (No.2), then overpipe the No.3 line (No.2).

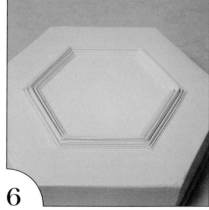

6
Pipe a line beside the inside and outside lines (No.2), then overpipe the No.2 line (No.1).

7
Pipe dots in groups of 6 around the inside and outside of the piped design (No.0).

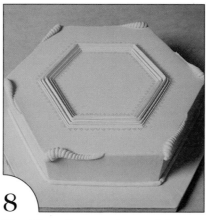

8
Pipe 'S' scrolls around part of the cake-top edge, as shown (No.44).

9
Pipe 'C' scrolls adjoining each 'S' scroll (No.44).

10
Pipe a heart shape adjoining the scrolls, as shown (No.44).

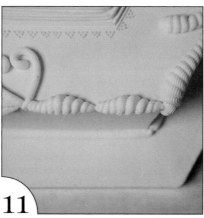

11
Fill in the remaining cake-top edge with piped spiral shells (No.44).

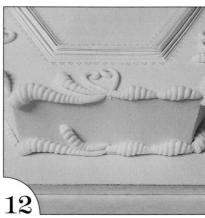

12
Repeat the cake-top edge design around the cake-base (omitting the heart design) (No.44).

13
Overpipe the scrolls and hearts, as shown (No.3).

14
Overpipe the scrolls and hearts, as shown (No.2).

15
Overpipe the scrolls and hearts, as shown (No.1).

16
Pipe scalloped lines around the cake-sides (No.2). Pipe a line below, then against the No.2 line (No.1).

17
Pipe dots in groups of 6, beneath the scalloped lines on the cake-sides (No.0).

18
Pipe a scalloped line around the cake board (No.2). Pipe a line beside, then overpipe the No.2 line (No.1).

19
Fix artificial decorations to each cake-side, in the position shown. Pipe dots along scallops (No.0).

20
Pipe inscription of choice onto the cake-top and fix decorations of choice.

21
Fix a flower to each corner, then complete by fixing a velvet ribbon around the edge of the cake board.

1 Using the template as a guide, pipe palm trees onto waxed paper, as shown. Leave to dry for 24 hours.

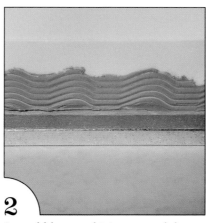

2 Spread blue royal icing around the base of the cake-sides and then form waves with a serrated scraper.

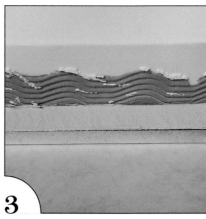

3 Brush white royal icing onto the waves to simulate surf. Spread royal icing over cake board and stipple to create a sand effect.

4 Using the template as a guide, pipe the outline of the sailor onto the cake-top, using royal icing (No.1).

5 Complete the outline of the sailor, as shown (No.1).

6 Pipe inscription of choice onto cake-top (No.1).

7 Pipe a palm tree on each side of the sailor (No.1).

8 Pipe grasses, fruit and foreground in royal icing (No.1).

9 Make assorted pebbles from sugarpaste and fix to cake board. Carefully remove the dry palm trees from the waxed paper and fix.

TEMPLATES

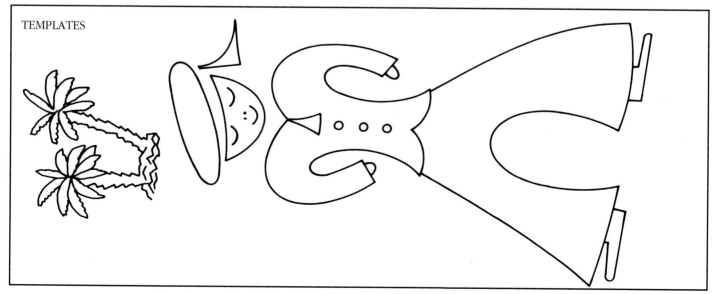

ELEANOR

1
Using the templates as guides, outline and flood-in on waxed paper: 1 glass, 2 large and 8 small elephants. Leave to dry for 24 hours.

2
Pipe bulbs on waxed paper (No.2). Cover in coloured granulated sugar. Leave to dry 24 hours. Decorate glass and fix to cake-top. Fix bubbles.

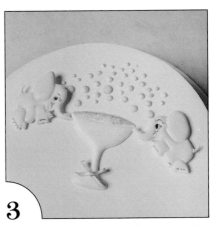

3
Paint the detail on the elephants with edible food colouring. Fix the large elephants to the cake-top, positioning as shown.

4

Pipe inscription of choice (No.1) and then decorate with tracery (No.0).

5

Fix the small elephants to the cake-side in pairs. Fix additional bubbles and a bow to link elephant trunks.

6

Pipe 'C' scrolls two-thirds of the way round the cake-top edge (No.42).

7

Pipe shells along the remaining cake-top edge, and around the cake-base (No.42).

8

Overpipe each scroll (No.2), then pipe a line beside each cake-top scroll (No.2), as shown.

9

Fix bubbles onto the cake board and then decorate the edge of the board with tracery (No.0).

TEMPLATES

1

To create a snow effect, finely stipple a dry coated cake with a sponge.

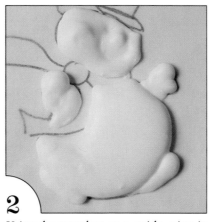

2

Using the template as a guide, pipe in the parts of the snowmen shown onto waxed paper with royal icing.

3

Fill in the remaining parts and leave to dry for 24 hours.

4 Paint in the features and decorate the hats and scarves.

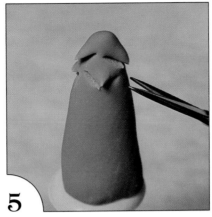

5 To make the Christmas trees, snip cones of sugarpaste from top to base, as shown.

6 Remove the snowmen from the waxed paper and fix onto the cake-top.

7 Fix the trees onto the cake-top and pipe on the snow. Pipe and decorate inscription of choice (No.1).

8 Pipe and then overpipe 'S' and 'C' scrolls on 2 sides of the cake (No's 7, 3 and 2). Stipple snow on the remaining sides. Fix the trees.

9 Make and fix sugarpaste snowballs onto the cake-top and cake board.

TEMPLATES

BRUSH EMBROIDERY

Brush embroidery is a delicate technique for creating pictures using a piping tube and a fine paintbrush. It is particularly appropriate for reproducing lace or flowers and is an ideal decoration for wedding or anniversary cakes. The technique can be used on sugarpaste, royal iced or buttercream coated cakes and is suitable for working in both royal icing and chocolate.

Appropriate colouring greatly enhances the finished effect. Highlighting and gentle shading of flower designs can considerably improve the overall appearance especially when attention is also paid to the texture and the natural fall of light. Consistently highlighting one side of a petal or leaf throughout the design will remove the 'flat' effect and will give the impression of light falling from a particular direction. Observing, and reproducing, the natural texture, such as leaf veins, or colouring a deeper shade at the base of a petal, for instance, will ensure the most realistic finish.

Considerable thought should be given to the colours used for brush embroidery. A white wedding cake, could, for example, look extremely elegant with a brushed white lace decoration, whilst a slightly deeper shade of a pale-iced cake colour would give a subtle play of light particularly if two tones are used, the darker one being the outer line. For a really dramatic effect, white icing on a dark cake, or dark icing on a white cake, has tremendous impact. However, if plenty of time is available, an exquisite effect can be created by combining several harmonising colours in one design.

When a suitable design has been selected, it should be transferred to the cake (see p.33) and the design worked from the outside towards the centre, concentrating on a very small area at a time. Freshly made royal icing, to which one teaspoon of piping gel has been added for every four tablespoons of icing, is the easiest medium to work in, as the gel reduces crusting and the icing remains workable for longer. Icing can be coloured before use, painted with edible food colouring, or dusted with petal dust when completed. If using several different colours of icing, an appropriate number of tubes and bags will be required.

A fine writing tube (No.1) is used for the outer line, with a finer, inner, line if necessary. The icing is then immediately stroked towards the centre with a fine, damp (but not too wet) paintbrush so that a film of icing covers the design, outlined by a firm edge. The brush should be at a 40° angle and used with a long, smooth stroke to avoid ridges. The icing film will be lighter as it draws towards the centre. If necessary the outer line can be overpiped to give a more defined edge to petals, etc. When working on leaves, veins can either be brushed out with a wet paintbrush, or piped on with a fine tube. Always remember that coloured icing will be almost impossible to remove completely, so extreme care should be taken both with colour and positioning of the icing.

GRANDAD

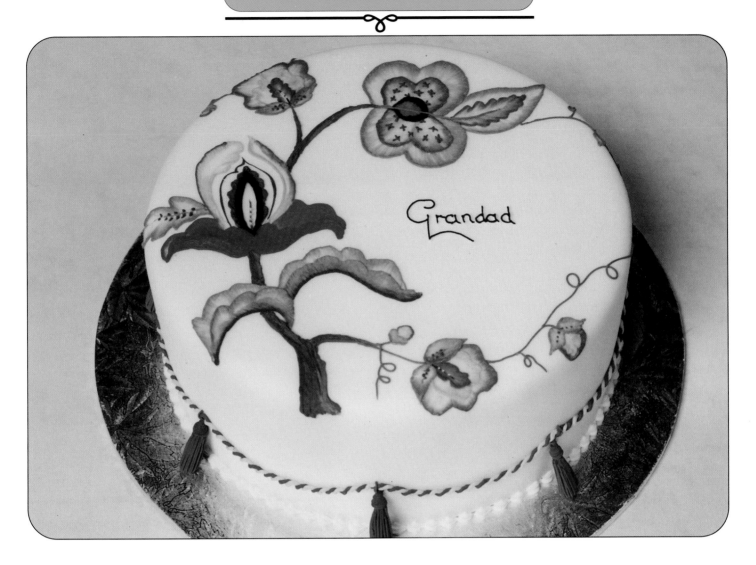

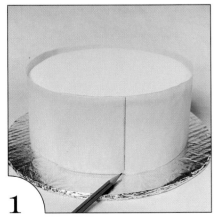

1

Leave a covered cake to dry for 4 days. Wrap a strip of greaseproof paper around the cake-side and mark exact circumference. Do not remove spare.

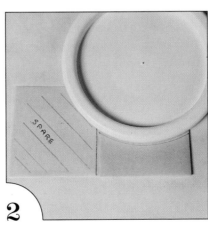

2

Excluding spare, fold paper in half. Repeat to make 8 sections. Mark 4cm (1½") up fold line. Cut scallops between each mark using a round object.

3

Trim spare paper to fit behind scallops and wrap around cake, overlapping spare. Fix with sticky tape. Scratch mark scallops. Remove paper.

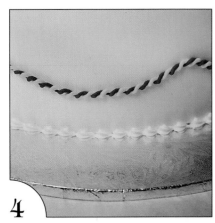

4

Using royal icing in alternate colours, pipe a rope on the cake-side following the scratched line (No.2). Pipe shells around the cake-base (No.5).

5

Insert cocktail sticks into wide ends of eight 2.5cm (1") pastillage cones. When dry, pipe tassels (No.1 or 0). When dry, pipe knot on top (No.1).

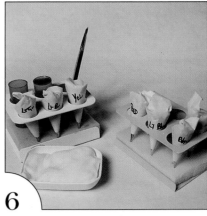

6

Mix all the colours of royal icing required for the floral design. Fill and mark each piping bag.

7

Transfer design to cake-top, marking outer edge and main lines. Pipe branches and stems (No.1). Paint texture in food colouring.

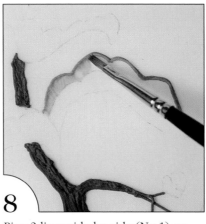

8

Pipe 2 lines side by side (No.1) on the first leaf. Brush down towards the next outline.

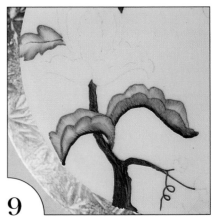

9

Repeat step 8 and then complete leaf by outlining base of leaf and brushing up towards centre for each leaf.

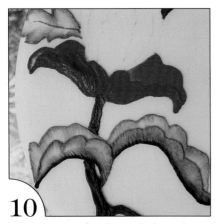

10

Repeat step 8 for the curled petals and then pipe over the first layer to build up thickness.

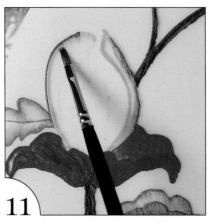

11

Pipe 2 lines in contrasting colours (No.1). Immediately brush over the lines to merge the colours.

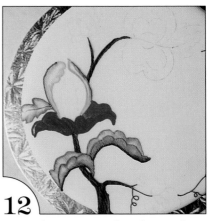

12

Pipe 2 lines to complete the petal outline (No.1) and brush, as in step 11.

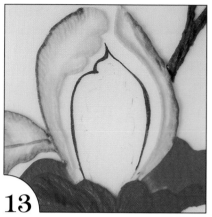

13 Paint the outline, as shown, using edible food colouring or a food pen.

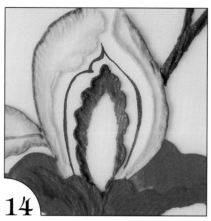

14 Pipe 2 lines in the centre of the flower and brush (No.1).

15 Complete the flower and leaf with piped lines and dots (No.1), as shown.

16 Repeat steps 8-9 to form the leaf shown.

17 Repeat steps 8-9 to form the second flower, and colour wash the centre.

18 Pipe and brush a black line around flower centre. Pipe a line across centre of flower to complete stem and leaf vein (No.1). Pipe crosses.

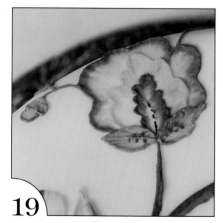

19 Repeat steps 16-18 to complete the third flower.

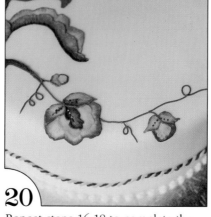

20 Repeat steps 16-18 to complete the small flower.

21 Fix a tassel between each scallop of rope, as shown.

TEMPLATE

ORLENA

1 Using a non-toxic pencil, trace the template, as shown. Re-trace design on reverse of paper so that it can be transferred to the cake-top.

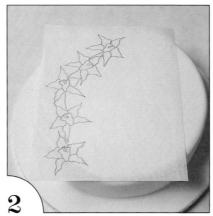

2 Place the tracing onto a dry covered cake and very lightly trace the design onto the cake-top.

3 Mix approximately 1 teaspoon of piping gel with 4 tablespoons of royal icing and brush embroider the orchids.

4 Before the icing dries, lightly brush the orchid with a second colour, adding dots in the centre, as shown, with food colouring.

5 Continue to brush embroider each orchid in the same way as steps 3-4.

6 Cut a strip of sugarpaste to fit the circumference of the cake. Frill with a cocktail stick and fix to cake-base using cool boiled water.

7 Cut a second strip in white sugarpaste and frill with a cocktail stick. Fix as in step 6, just above the green frill.

8 Pipe shells of royal icing along the edge of the top frill, as shown (No.2).

9 Complete the cake by fixing 6 miniature orchids to the cake-top and one on the cake board, as shown in the main picture.

TEMPLATE

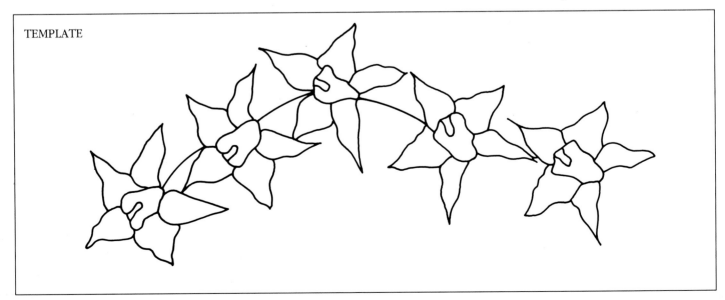

1 Cut a 13cm (5") square cake diagonally. Fix to an 18cm (7") cake. Place on thin board cut to size. Cover in sugarpaste and place on a board.

2 Brush embroider the oak and maple leaves. Pipe tear-drops of royal icing along the outline of the maple leaves (No.1) and brush towards centre.

3 Brush embroider the ivy leaves and pipe in the stems (No.1). Brush in shadows and highlights with diluted food colourings.

193

4 Pipe a shell border around the cake-base (No.7) and then fix a ribbon band, as shown.

5 Using flower paste, make 2 oak leaves using template B; 3 ivy leaves using template C; and 1 ivy leaf using template D.

6 Cut out 1 small ivy leaf from flower paste. Cut off the two bottom lobes. Lay a length of fine moistened wire on the leaf and roll leaf around wire.

7 Using template A, cut maple leaves and snip diagonally around edges (twisting knife slightly while cutting to open up points). Wire and vein.

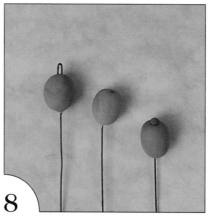

8 Make 3 acorns from paste balls. Push hooked wire into top. Conceal hook with paste ball. Leave to dry. Glaze with gum arabic solution.

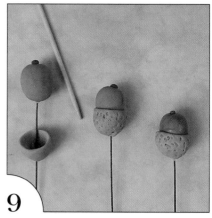

9 Hollow out a paste ball to make acorn cup. Thread onto wire. Fit acorn inside moistened cup. Texture with cocktail stick. Leave to dry.

10 Tape 1 oak, maple and ivy leaf into a spray. Bend wires at right angles just below ivy leaves. Repeat for a second spray. Tape sprays together.

11 Tape wired ivy leaves into a spray and then tape to the 2 leaf sprays.

12 Tape 3 acorns together and then tape into the centre of the spray. Trim wires and curl ends to neaten.

13

Fix spray to cake-top using a small piece of moistened sugarpaste. Neaten the back of the spray with a flat ribbon bow.

14

Decorate border by fixing unwired ivy leaves with royal icing around the cake-base. Pipe stems between the leaves (No.1).

15

Complete the cake by piping inscription of choice between brush embroidered sprays (No.1).

TEMPLATES

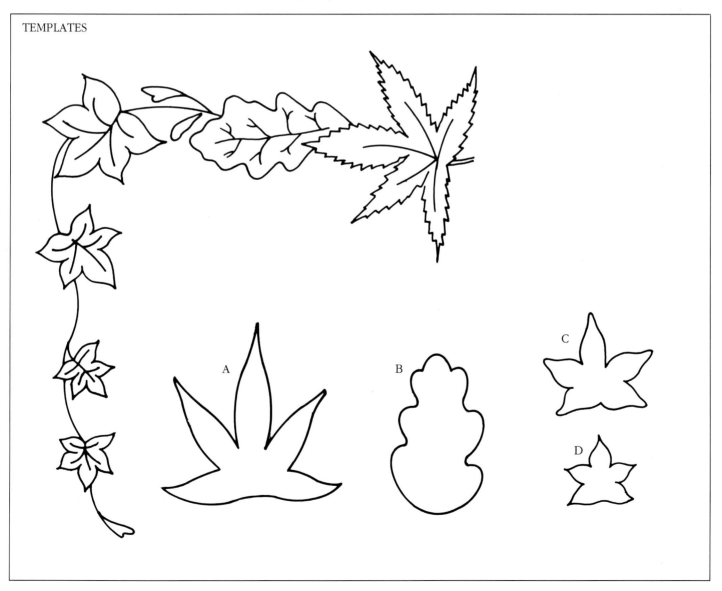

A

B

C

D

SUGARPASTE-COVERED CAKES

Many of the cakes in this book have been covered in sugarpaste, which produces a beautifully smooth and silky finish with flowing lines that require the minimum of decoration to create a stunning effect. Sugarpaste is an instant covering as it goes on in one operation, and can be bought ready-made if required. It is a very versatile medium as it colours and flavours easily and can be used for covering, decorating and modelling. Sugarpaste is ideal for creating novelty cakes, such as the Wind in the Willows (p.209), which require a touch of imagination and a little expertise; but is also an excellent medium for the beginner, with no practical experience or specialist tools to work in, as the elegant, yet extremely simple, design on p.198 illustrates. Sugarpaste can also be combined with royal icing to achieve a variety of effects, as can be seen from the delightful fairy cake on p.205 and the delicate crib on p.216. Royal icing lace (see p.212) adds a pretty touch and can be combined with frills or ribbon work.

Sugarpaste is applied to an almond paste or marzipan-covered cake which is completely dry. To ensure the best possible finish, the almond paste should be as level and smooth as possible. Use of a clear alcoholic liquor, such as vodka, bacardi or gin brushed over the almond paste, will have a sterilising effect which helps prevent the development of mould or fermentation. (Do not use coloured alcohol liquors such as brandy or rum as this may discolour the sugarpaste). Instructions for covering a cake in almond and sugarpaste are shown on p.22. The sugarpaste for covering should be made at least 24 hours before use and kept in an airtight container in a cool place (but not a refrigerator) until required. If the paste is found to be too dry to roll out or will not mould easily, add a little white fat or egg-white to the mixture. If the paste is too sticky, a little cornflour or icing sugar can be added to the mixture. Sugarpaste should be rolled out on an icing sugar dusted surface.

When applying sugarpaste to the cake, great care should be taken not to trap any air under the sugarpaste. Work from the centre of the cake, smoothing the sugarpaste with the flat of the hand and then polish with a smoother. If sharp edges are required, cover the cake with almond paste as described on p.24-25 and then create sharp edges and corners as described in step 9 on p.22. If an air bubble does appear under the surface, use a pin with a large coloured head to prick it, and then smooth again (ensuring that the pin is safely removed from the cake). If required, the cake board can also be covered with sugarpaste as shown in step 8 on p.22. The cake should then be left until a crust has formed on the surface. This normally takes 24 hours in a dry, warm room of (18°C/65°F). However, if the weather is very damp and humid extra time will obviously be required for drying.

If the sugarpaste is to be crimped or decorated with broderie anglaise (see p.23 and p.222) this should be carried out as soon as the cake has been covered. Ribbon insertion, however, is best carried out when the sugarpaste is dry (see p.23).

Colouring and Flavouring Sugarpaste

Sugarpaste should be coloured with edible paste food colouring as liquid may affect the texture. Dip a cocktail stick or skewer into the colour and then add a very small amount at a time to the paste. Knead well until the colour is thoroughly mixed. (To create a marbled effect, mix until streaky and then roll out). To check if the colour has been thoroughly mixed in, the paste should be rolled out thinly and an even colour should be seen. Sufficient sugarpaste should be coloured at one time for all the tiers of a cake as it will be virtually impossible to match the colour at a later date.

An extremely creative effect can be achieved by graduating the colour of a tiered cake (see p.239). White sugarpaste is added to the first base colour to produce a decreasing strength of shade and repeated until an almost white colour is made for the final tier.

It is most important to protect coloured sugarpaste from strong light, therefore it should be stored in a sealed container. When the cake has been decorated, it should be returned to a cardboard box and must be kept at a constant temperature of 18°C/65°F.

Flavouring sugarpaste can counteract the sweetness of the paste. Almond essence produces a very agreeable flavour in almost any colour paste but flavouring can also be linked to colour. Oil of peppermint is ideal for white paste, raspberry for pinks, and the citrus flavours for orange and lemon colours. For blue cakes, use vanilla essence. When flavouring, remember to use sparingly and check for taste before covering the cake.

Crimping

Crimping is an extremely effective decoration for sugarpaste-coated cakes and a variety of crimper shapes are available, although crimping can be improvised with kitchen tools - as can be seen on p.199. It should be borne in mind that, once a design has been crimped, it cannot be removed from the surface so beginners should practise on a sugarpaste-covered 'dummy' cake.

Crimping must be carried out as soon as the cake has been covered, otherwise the sugarpaste will crack. Clean, dry, crimpers should be lightly greased with white fat or dipped in cornflour to prevent sticking. When working, hold the crimper at right angles to the cake and gently push into the cake before squeezing the crimper. Release the pressure and then remove from the paste.

Frills

Frills, which are usually attached when the sugarpaste covering has dried, look very attractive on celebration cakes for many occasions. The technique is illustrated on p.36 and the frill should be attached by moistening with boiled, cooled water. The join can then be decorated with royal icing. By rolling out the paste extremely thinly, a translucent effect is achieved. When using graduated shades, the thinner the frill the more the colours can shine through the layers. Frills can also look very effective when lightly dusted at the edges with confectioners' dusting powder.

Ribbon Work

Ribbons can be used in a variety of ways on sugarpaste-coated cakes, and p.23 illustrates some of the effects that can be produced by ribbon insertion into the sugarpaste. Ribbons can, however, be used round a cake-side, as illustrated on p.200 and 217, or as bands across the top. They are often used for decorating floral sprays or for disguising the back of top ornaments. The most appropriate ribbon to use is double-sided polyester satin with woven edges as this does not fray and is available in a wide range of colours and widths. It holds its shape well if used to form loops and bows, and looks attractive from either side. Some ribbons designed for gift wrapping can also create an unusual effect on a cake.

When attaching ribbon around the side of a cake, mark the position carefully by scratching a line at the appropriate height. Place the cake on a turntable, then pipe a dot of royal icing onto the cake and fix the end of the ribbon with a large-headed pin. Turn the turntable slowly, positioning the ribbon as you work, and fix the ribbon with dots of royal icing. Cut off the ribbon, leaving a slight overlap and fix into place with royal icing and a pin. When the icing is dry, remove the pins.

Ribbon insertion, which creates the effect of a ribbon woven in and out of the cake covering, should be carried out on sugarpaste which has dried to a crust, but is not too hard. The design should be marked on the cake and sufficient pieces of ribbon cut to fill the spaces. When cutting, ensure that the ribbon is slightly longer than the gap to be filled so that the ends can be tucked well in. The ribbon is inserted using a fine blade or a long pin. Once inserted, the ribbon should not require further fixing.

Embossing

Embossing, an extremely easy technique for cake decorators to use, creates an intricate pattern. It must be carried out on freshly applied sugarpaste. Place a plastic doyley on the cake-top, carefully centering the design (it may be necessary for an assistant to hold the doyley in place). Then place a rolling pin at one side and, with a firm, continuous movement, roll across the top of the doyley. Carefully remove the doyley. The cake can then be decorated as required with flowers, etc, or a light colouring of confectioners' dusting powder; and a ribbon, or frill, attached to the sides.

DAISY

1 Cover a 20.5cm (8") round cake with almond paste. Fix the cake to a board, as shown.

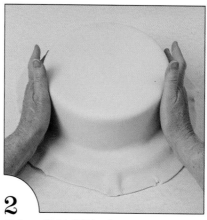

2 Colour 905g (2lb) of sugarpaste. Roll out the sugarpaste and cover the cake and board, as shown. Smooth the paste with the palm of the hands.

3 Smooth the sugarpaste onto the board and trim away excess with a sharp knife.

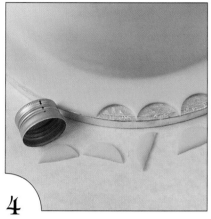

4 Using a bottle-top, cut out scallops of sugarpaste around the edge of the board, as shown.

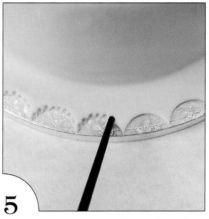

5 Decorate the edge of the scallops by pressing the end of a paintbrush handle, or similar tool, into the sugarpaste.

6 Mark a circle in the sugarpaste by pressing gently, but evenly, with a saucepan lid which should be slightly smaller than the cake-top.

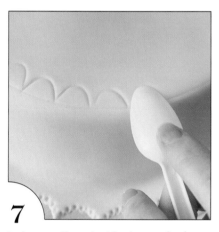

7 Indent scallops inside the marked circle using the tip of a teaspoon, as shown.

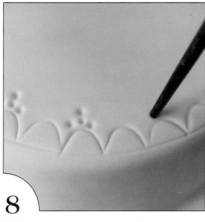

8 Make dots by indenting the sugarpaste with the end of a paint-brush handle. Leave to dry for 2 hours, or until a crust forms.

9 Roll out a small piece of sugarpaste. Cut 2 leaves using template A and 7 petals using B. Mark veins with a cocktail stick.

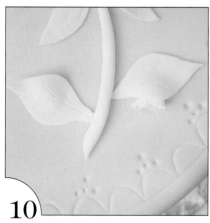

10 Make a stem from sugarpaste and fix on cake-top with leaves and petals. Curl leaves slightly, supporting with tissue paper until dry.

11 Remove tissue paper. Tie a ribbon around the cake-side and add greeting of choice.

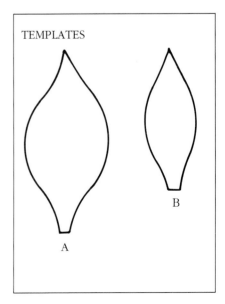

TEMPLATES

A

B

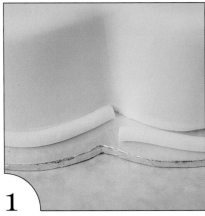

1 Cover a cake with sugarpaste. Make long rolls of sugarpaste and fix, as a border, around the cake-base, as shown. Neaten joins.

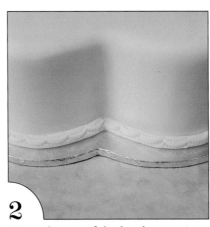

2 Crimp the top of the border, starting at the sides of each scallop and working towards the centres. Adjust spacing where necessary.

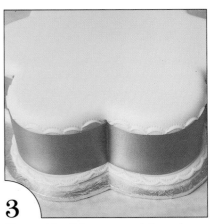

3 Fix a wide ribbon around the cake-sides. Crimp the sugarpaste above the ribbon, as shown.

4 Using the template as a guide, cut out a plaque from pastillage. Cut slots in the plaque, long enough to accommodate the width of narrow ribbon.

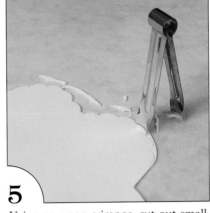

5 Using an open crimper, cut out small scallops around the edge of the plaque. Leave the plaque to dry on a flat surface for 24 hours.

6 Make a large rose, using 5-6 rows of petals (see p.104). Leave to dry for 24 hours.

7 Cut out, wire and vein rose leaves (see p.105). 2 large, 2 medium and 1 small rose leaf required. Leave to dry for 24 hours.

8 Dust the rose petals with petal dust, as shown.

9 Tape the leaves into a spray and dust with petal dust.

10 Wire the leaf spray behind the rose. Add a bow of ribbon if required.

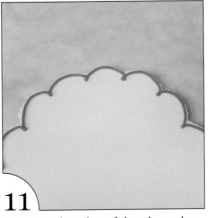

11 Decorate the edge of the plaque by piping with royal icing, as shown (No.1).

12 Thread the narrow ribbon through the slots. Pipe inscription of choice (No.1). Using the template as a guide, pipe braille as shown (No.1).

13 Tie the spray onto the plaque with narrow ribbon. This will enable the rose to be removed.

14 Using the template as a guide, prick the dots onto the cake-top. Pipe a small dot of royal icing onto each mark (No.1).

15 Fix the plaque to the cake-top, using a little royal icing.

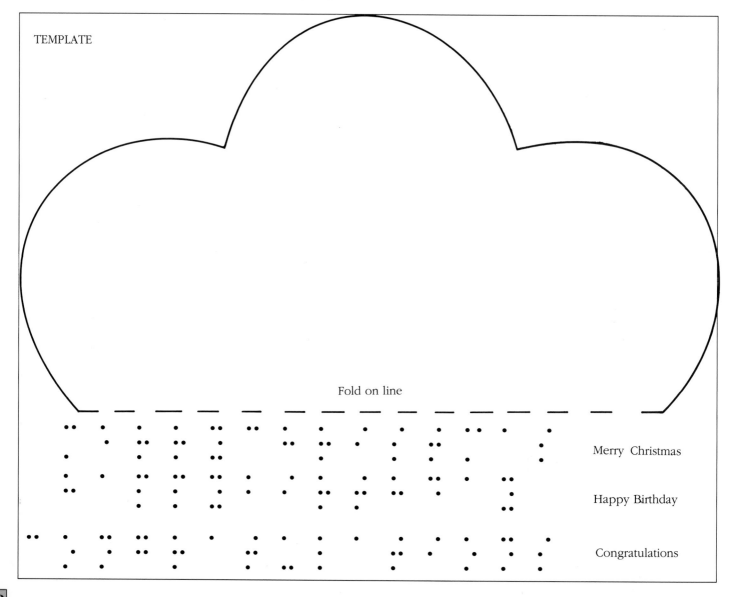

TEMPLATE

Fold on line

Merry Christmas

Happy Birthday

Congratulations

SPLODGER

1 Using a round cutter, cut off small pieces at the top of a round sponge to form the body, as shown.

2 Place one of the off-cuts near the top of the sponge to form the mouth, as shown. Coat the whole sponge in buttercream.

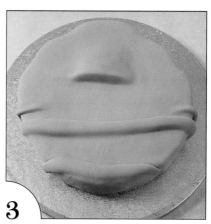

3 Roll out sugarpaste and immediately cover the sponge, carefully smoothing over the mouth, forming folds on the lower part of the body.

4

Trim away the excess sugarpaste and smooth the sides. Pipe royal icing shells around the cake-base (No.42), as shown.

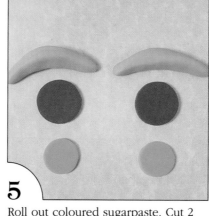

5

Roll out coloured sugarpaste. Cut 2 discs in orange and 2 slightly smaller discs in red for the eyes. Form 2 rolls of green sugarpaste for the eyebrows.

6

Moisten and fix the eyes and eyebrows to the head, as shown.

7

Make a cone of sugarpaste to form the nose. Flatten the wide end and indent twice, to form the nostrils.

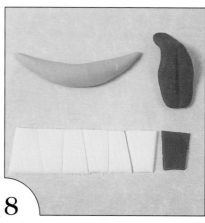

8

Make the various shapes shown to form the mouth pieces, using sugarpaste to form the lip, tongue and teeth.

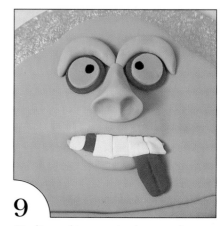

9

Fix lip and tongue to the mouth before fixing teeth and gap, as shown.

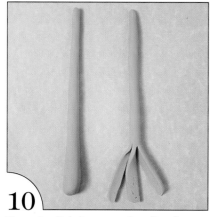

10

Form 2, slightly tapered, rolls of sugarpaste to form the arms. Cut 3 fingers in each of the wider ends and smooth the outer edges.

11

Fix the arms to the cake-side, bending at the elbows, as shown. Fix the fingers onto the face and body.

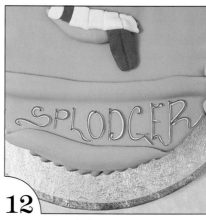

12

Pipe name of choice (No.1) onto the body, as shown.

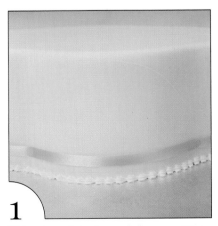

1 Using template A, mark lace position around and over cake 6mm (¼") from edge. Pipe shells around cake-base (No.5). Fix 1cm (½") ribbon.

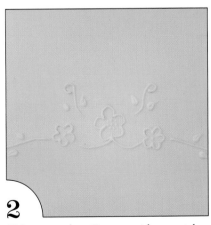

2 Using template F as a guide, scratch mark the embroidery pattern on three side panels. Pipe the design in royal icing (No.1).

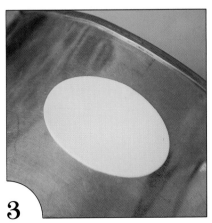

3 Using template B as a guide, cut out a small oval plaque from Mexican paste and lay on the side of the cake tin. Leave to dry for 24 hours.

4
Using templates E, outline and flood-in fairies on waxed paper. Leave to dry 24 hours. Remove from paper and repeat on reverse side.

5
Make the baby's head, hand and arm from Mexican paste. Cut out 30 small and 5 medium pink and white blossoms. Leave to dry.

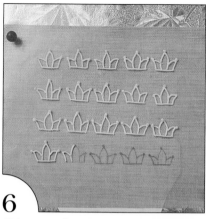

6
Using template D as guide, pipe lace onto waxed paper in rows of 5 for easy counting (No.0). 100 pieces required. Leave to dry for 24 hours.

7
Tape together nine 9cm (3½") strands of 26 gauge wire, 2cm (¾ ") up from bottom. Divide ends into 3. Tape to form roots. Spread wires and trim.

8
Pipe leaves along the length of each branch. Pipe in yellowish-green gooseberries (No.1).

9
Dust edge of oval plaque. Cut a large oval from Mexican paste and frill edge. Lay on side of cake tin and fix small oval in centre. Leave to dry.

10
Using a fine paintbrush, apply royal icing to area within hairline of fairies and spread icing to give simulated hair. Paint in highlights.

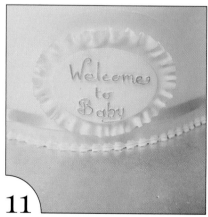

11
Dust the edges of the frill. Pipe inscription of choice (No.1) and fix completed plaque to the centre front of the cake.

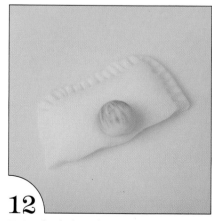

12
Paint the baby's hair. Make a pillow from sugarpaste and decorate edge. Indent pillow to take baby's head and fix to cake-top.

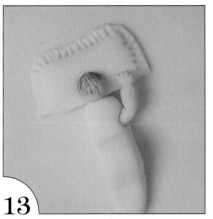

13
Slightly flatten a roll of sugarpaste and form a hump in the centre. Place below the pillow. Position the baby's arm and fix, as shown.

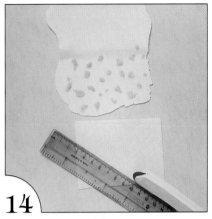

14
Roll out a piece of sugarpaste. Lay tiny pieces of pink sugarpaste on top, fold and re-roll. Fold and roll to achieve a soft mottled effect.

15
Cut blanket from mottled paste. Use a tracing wheel and ruler to create quilt. Frill edge. Place over baby and turn back top edge.

16
Mark positions on cake-top for fairies' extensions. Cut slots. Fix fairies into the slots with royal icing. Leave to dry for 30 minutes.

17
Carefully bend a fine white wire so that it will lie behind the sitting fairy, reaching up behind her hand.

18
From just above her hand, curve the wire until it lies in front of standing fairy's hands. Bend to lie along cake-top. Pipe grass (No.1).

19
Once the wire fits, trim both ends so that approximately 2.5cm (1") lies on the cake-top. Fix with royal icing. Fix blossoms to wire and cake-top.

20
Position and fix gooseberry bush onto the cake-top.

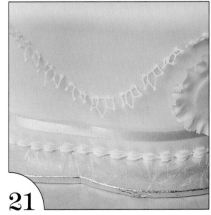

21
Complete the cake by fixing the lace along the scored guide line, as shown. Note: Remove the wires before cutting the cake.

TEMPLATES

WIND IN
THE WILLOWS

1 Fix a roll of sugarpaste onto the cake-top to form edge of pond. Cover the cake in the usual way, as shown.

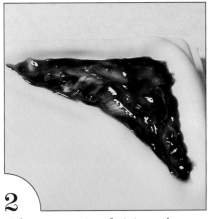

2 Colour a quantity of piping gel to resemble water and fill the pond.

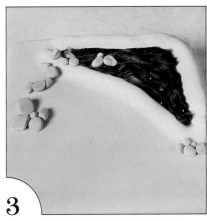

3 Make several different shaped stones from sugarpaste and fix onto the cake-top as shown.

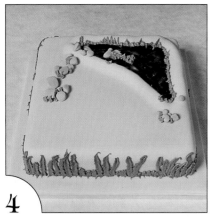

4

Using a leaf bag, pipe long upright leaves, in royal icing, around the cake-side to form reeds.

5

Roughly mix 2 colours of sugarpaste and make 3 rolls for fish. Pinch out tails and fins and cut with scissors. Use tip of piping tube to mark scales.

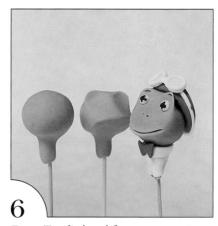

6

Form Toad's head from sugarpaste. Pinch out brows, and across front to form mouth. Cut mouth. Make and fix hat, goggles, collar and tie.

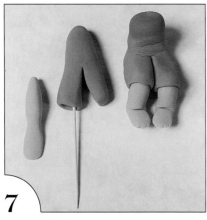

7

Cut a roll of sugarpaste (approximately half way down) and hollow out with a cocktail stick. Make, insert and fix legs. Bend feet and waist.

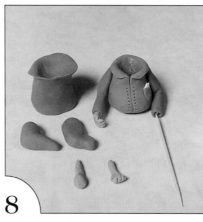

8

Make body from sugarpaste and hollow out. Thin top edge, fold down collar and mark front to form jacket. Make and fix arms and hands.

9

Bend the body and legs and fix to a sugarpaste stone. Leave to dry. Remove cocktail stick from head and fix onto body with royal icing.

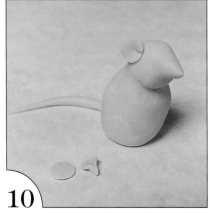

10

Make a roll of sugarpaste, pointed at one end. Bend slightly to form head and body. Flatten 2 paste balls and crease for ears. Make and fix a tail.

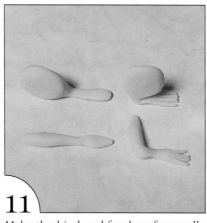

11

Make the hind and forelegs from rolls of sugarpaste and cut claws with a craft knife.

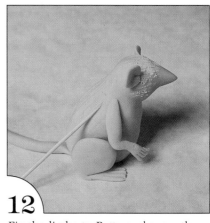

12

Fix the limbs to Ratty and score the whole surface with a cocktail stick to resemble fur.

13

Paint Ratty's body with food colouring. Paint in the nose, eyes and claws.

14

Make Mole in a similar way as Ratty. Pipe lines to form Mole's glasses onto waxed paper and leave to dry. Fix glasses to nose, as shown.

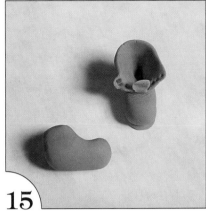

15

Make an old boot from sugarpaste and cut the sole with a craft knife. Mark eyelets with a cocktail stick.

16

Make 2 fishing rods, uprights and firewood from sugarpaste, as shown.

17

Fix the uprights and fishing rods beside the pond using royal icing. Place the fish in the pond, as shown.

18

Fix Mole and Ratty to the cake-top. Pipe fishing line along rod and into pond (No.1). Make an old tin can and fix boot and tin to line ends.

19

Fix Toad and rock to cake-top. Pipe flames onto cake surface and then fix the firewood.

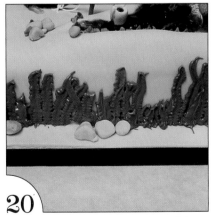

20

Fix a ribbon around the edge of the cake board. Make and fix stones around the cake-base, as shown.

21

Pipe inscription of choice onto one corner of the cake (No.1).

DANIELLE

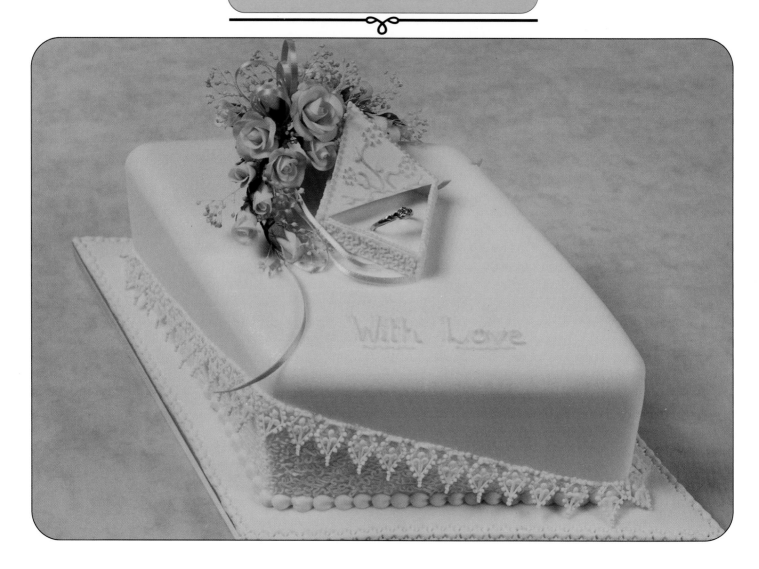

1

Using the template as a guide, pipe approximately 60 pieces of lace work in royal icing onto waxed paper (No.1). Leave to dry for 24 hours.

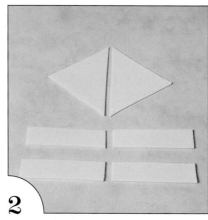

2

Roll out Mexican paste and cut out the ring box, using the templates as guides. Leave to dry for 24 hours.

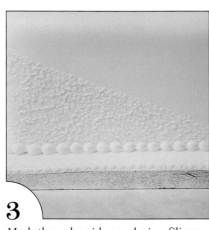

3

Mark the cake-sides and pipe filigree, as shown (No.0). Pipe shells around the cake-base (No.2).

4

Fix rows of lace just above the piped filigree, using royal icing (No.0).

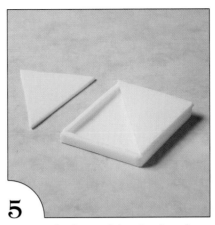

5

Cut out the base of the ring box from Mexican paste, making it slightly smaller than the lid. Fix sides and 1 lid with royal icing.

6

Pipe decorations onto the ring box and lid, as shown (No.1). Push a ring into the paste while it is still soft.

7

Fix the lid with royal icing and support until dry. Add colour to the piped decorations using lustre dusting powder.

8

Fix the ring box to the cake-top using royal icing. Add a spray of flowers or other decoration of choice.

9

Pipe inscription of choice (No.2). Overpipe the inscription (No.1).

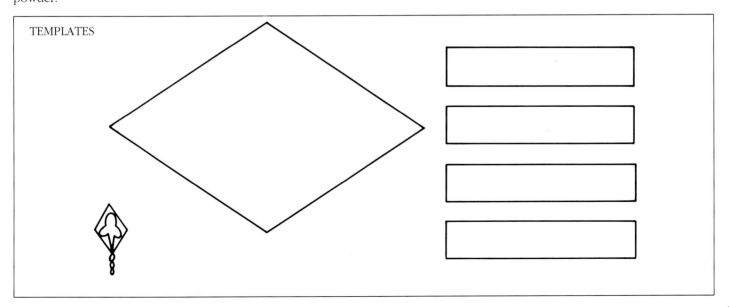

TEMPLATES

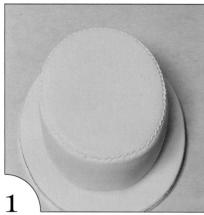

1 Cover an oval cake and board in sugarpaste and crimp the cake-top edge, as shown.

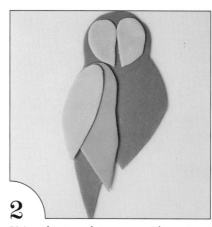

2 Using the template as a guide, cut out the owl shapes from sugarpaste and fix onto the cake-top with cooled boiled water.

3 Fix 2 circles of sugarpaste for the eyes and pipe the centres in royal icing (No.3). Cut a diamond shape and fix to face to form beak.

4 Mould a tree, with branches, from sugarpaste. Fix the tree to the cake-base, arranging it up the cake-side and across the cake-top, as shown.

5 Using a leaf cutter, cut approximately 18 leaves from sugarpaste and fix to the branches. Dust leaves with confectioners' dusting powder.

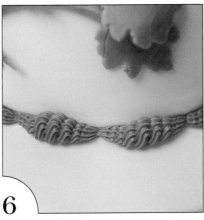

6 Pipe spiral shells around the cake-base (No.7). Decorate board with fallen leaves.

TEMPLATES

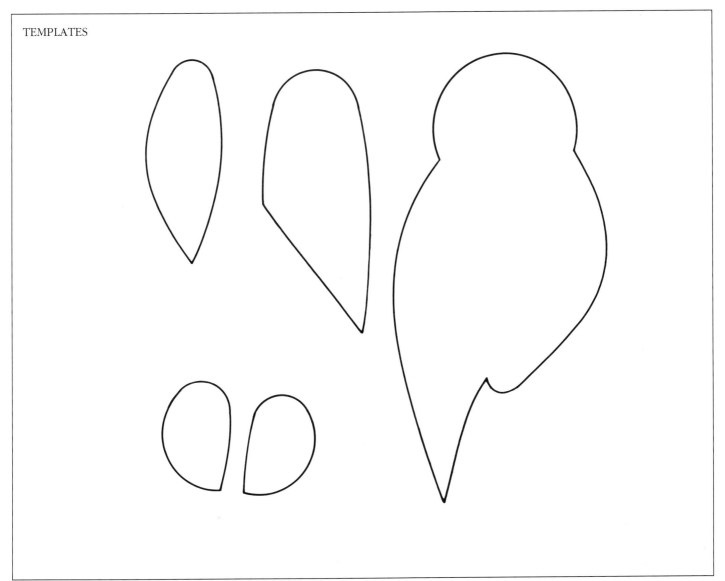

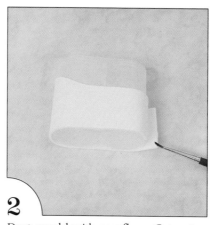

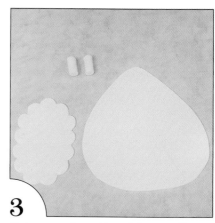

1
Tape together 2 plastic cylinders 3cm (1¼") in diameter for mould. Wrap a 30.5cm (12") strip of waxed paper tightly around and secure with tape.

2
Dust mould with cornflour. Cut out crib body from paste, using template A. Wrap around mould. Moisten edges to join. Leave to dry 24 hours.

3
Using templates B and C, cut crib base and plaque. Cut 6mm (¼") diameter roll of paste into 2 x 2cm (¾") lengths. Leave to dry 24 hours.

4 Make flowers and leaves from flower paste, using a variety of cutters. Approximately 5 large and 16 small flowers required.

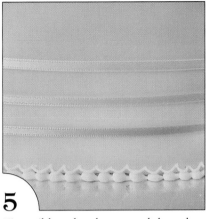

5 Fix a ribbon border around the cake-side, as shown. Pipe plain shells around cake-base (No.2). Pipe tiny loops above the shells (No.1).

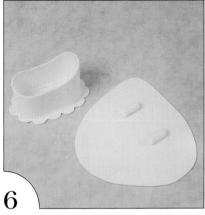

6 Remove crib from mould and fix to base with royal icing. Fix crib runners to plaque in positions marked on template. Leave to dry.

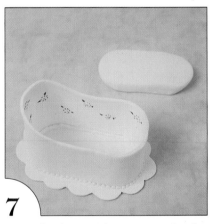

7 Using food pens, decorate inside of crib with tiny flowers. Roll sugarpaste to 6mm (¼") thick and cut out mattress using template D.

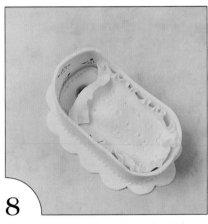

8 Fix the mattress into the crib. Make, fix and decorate pillow, baby's head and a blanket, as shown.

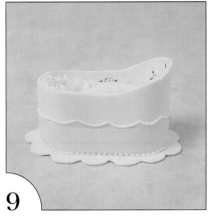

9 Place a 1cm (½") strip of paper around the crib. Pipe scallops above this guide to match scallops around crib-base (No.0).

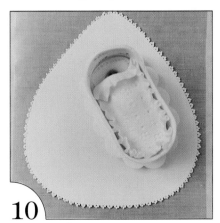

10 Fix crib to runners using royal icing. Stand plaque on a non-stick surface and decorate edge with a piped dots (No.0). Leave to dry for 1 hour.

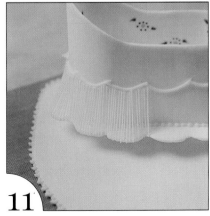

11 Pipe extension lines from below the piped scallops to edge of crib-base (No.00).

12 Pipe a line against the No.0 line (No.0). Repeat rows of lines. Ensure that each piped row is dry before adding the next.

13
Pipe extension lines from crib-top to piped bridge. Neaten top edge and bottom of extensions with piped shells (No.0). Decorate extensions.

14
Pipe stems directly onto cake-top (No.1) and fix flowers and leaves, as shown.

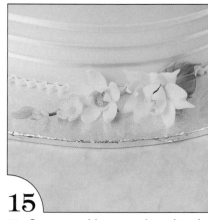

15
Fix flowers and leaves to board in the position shown in main photograph. Pipe the baby's name (No.0).

TEMPLATES

A

B

C

D

JANINE

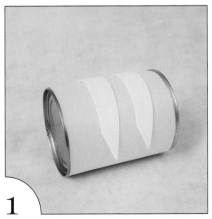

1

Using template A, cut 2 pieces from Mexican paste and leave to dry over a cylinder 5cm (2") in diameter. Allow the last 1cm (½") to hang straight.

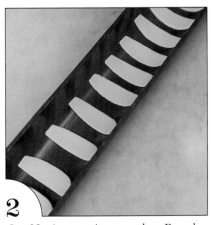

2

Cut 28 pieces using template B and lay in a cornflour-dusted former. Leave to dry. Clean curved edges with a knife, if necessary.

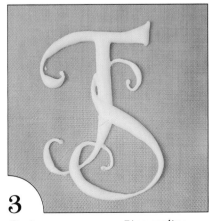

3

Design a monogram. Pipe outline (No.0) and flood-in onto waxed paper. Leave to dry for 24 hours.

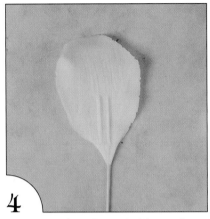

4 Using template C, cut 2 side petals from flower paste, leaving thick paste at base. Thin edges. Insert 30 gauge wire at base and pinch raised veins.

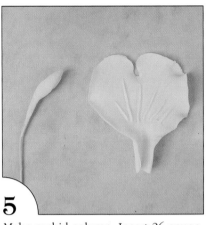

5 Make orchid column. Insert 26 gauge wire. Cut petal (D). Frill edges. Pinch veins. Moisten base, wrap around column to fix. Dry upside down.

6 Cut 3 back petals using template G. Pinch in raised veins. Thin edges and insert wire. Curl petals back. Leave to dry. Dust and highlight veins.

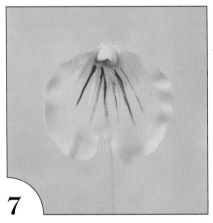

7 Dust yellow flash in D petal and paint red lines between veins.

8 Tape 2 C petals and fix to column behind D petal. Tape in 3 G petals. Trim wires and tape stem.

9 Make 10 honeysuckle flowers, small green and large pink buds to complete sprays. Make 16 forget-me-nots. Leave to dry.

10 Cut out butterfly wings templates E and F. Thin edges and cup slightly. Leave to dry before painting wing designs. Dust with silver lustre.

11 Curl stamens for antennae. Push wire through waxed paper and pipe bodies over wire. Push wings and antennae into bodies, support until dry.

12 Position and fix monogram onto cake-top. Decorate with piped curved lines (No.1), and flowers if required.

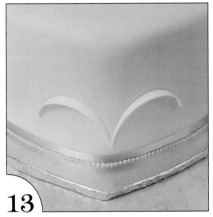

13

Fix ribbon around cake-base. Pipe shells, as shown (No.0). Push scalloped border sections into cake-side, beginning with large curves.

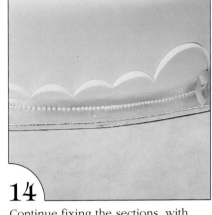

14

Continue fixing the sections, with each touching, as shown. Fix a ribbon bow to the centre front below the points of the large curves.

15

Make 2 ribbon tails, 24 finger loops and 4 double bows. Tape up a pair of sprays using a selection of flowers, buds and finger loops.

16

Carefully remove butterflies. Pipe under bodies to neaten, if required. Tape wires together, adding a 24 gauge wire to strengthen.

17

Make a centre spray by taping 4 double bows to form a circle of loops and tails. Add a few flowers and buds. Tape butterflies into spray.

18

Tape centre spray between side sprays. Tape in last orchid. Trim wires, tape and neaten stem. Fix spray to cake-top and fix with sugarpaste.

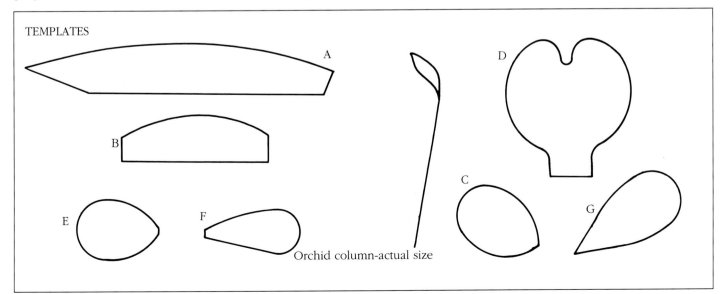

TEMPLATES

A

B

D

C

E

F

G

Orchid column-actual size

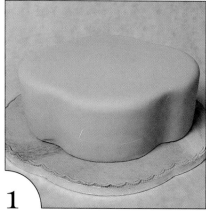

1

Cover a cake and board in sugarpaste. Crimp around edge of cake board. Scratch the cake-sides to mark guideline for frill.

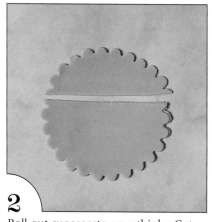

2

Roll out sugarpaste very thinly. Cut out 12 shapes using a small crimped cutter. Trim away the top third of each shape and discard.

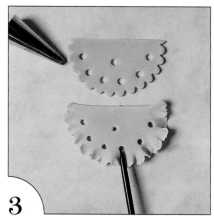

3

Punch out holes using a No.3 piping tube to make the broderie anglaise design. Frill the curved edge of each shape using a cocktail stick.

4

Fix each frill around the cake-side using a little cooled boiled water.

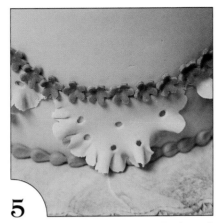

5

Mix sugarpaste to a darker shade and cut out medium sized blossoms. Fix the blossoms along the top edge of the frills.

6

Using royal icing in a contrasting colour, pipe a centre in each blossom (No.1). Pipe a circle around the punched holes in each frill.

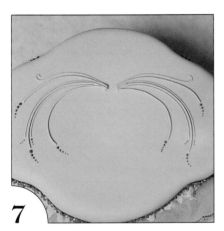

7

Pipe curved lines and a series of dots, as shown (No's.1 and 2).

8

Make and fix a tulle orchid (see p.129) and 2 sugar doves (see p.246) to the cake-top.

9

Pipe inscription of choice onto cake-top and fix further decorations, as shown.

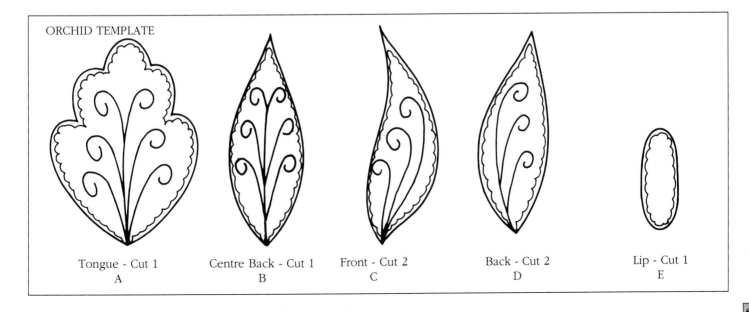

ORCHID TEMPLATE

Tongue - Cut 1
A

Centre Back - Cut 1
B

Front - Cut 2
C

Back - Cut 2
D

Lip - Cut 1
E

WEDDING CAKES

Wedding cakes offer an unrivalled opportunity for creative design and the display of cake artistry skills.

Size and Shape

The first design consideration is the shape and size of cake, which must be based on the number of portions required. It would be wasteful, for instance, to make a large three-tier cake for a small wedding party. On the other hand, an additional iced but undecorated cake may be required for a large, formal wedding. As it is traditional to save the small top tier for an anniversary or christening, the bottom tiers should be large enough to serve all the wedding guests. The table below indicates the approximate number of portions per size of cake, and the bride's preference for a tiered or single cake should also be taken into consideration before deciding on the final size, shape and design. Unusual shapes, such as hexagonal, petal or heart, can create added impact to a simple design by both the beginner and the experienced cake decorating enthusiast, and provide approximately the same number of portions as a round cake.

Portions

Round Portions		Square Portions	
13cm (5")	14	13cm (5")	16
15cm (6")	22	15cm (6")	27
18cm (7")	30	18cm (7")	40
20cm (8")	40	20cm (8")	54
23cm (9")	54	23cm (9")	90
25cm (10")	68	25cm (10")	90
30cm (12")	100	30cm (12")	134

Tiered cakes	Round	Square
3-tier 13,18,23cm (5,7,9")	98	126
3-tier 15,20,25cm (6,8,10")	130	171
2-tier 18 & 25cm (7 & 10")	98	130

Colour

Colour is also an important consideration as it is now fashionable to have a coloured, rather than the traditional white cake. The background colour may be selected to tone in with the bridal flowers, the bridesmaids' dresses or the bride's favourite colour. Too pale a shade should be avoided as it can look washed-out and insipid, and too harsh a colour may appear inappropriate. Remember that icing always dries a little darker than at first appears. A deep tone can look very sophisticated with paler, or white icing, and graduated tones can be very striking as in the three-tier cake on p.239.

It may be necessary to obtain colour swatches or sample flowers if specific colours are to be matched or toned. Once the basic colour scheme has been decided, there is then a need to consider whether the decoration is to be in toning shades of the same colour, or whether other colours are to be incorporated. Where deep or brilliant shades are introduced, as in sugar flowers for example, they should be kept to a minimum and used for small items only as otherwise they become overpowering.

Overall Design

The overall design of the cake can be formal, with the sharp lines of a royal iced cake which is particularly suitable if pillars are to be used; or the softer, gentler lines of a sugarpaste-covered cake, which is the most suitable for the flowing lines of modern cake stands or a single-tier cake.

Balance and harmony, with the correct proportions, are essential. If a sugar flower replica of the bridal bouquet, or a spray of the same flowers, is used for the top of the cake, the size of the cake will need to be sufficient for this not to overpower the finished effect. Here, a large, single-tier cake could be more effective than a tiered cake.

Inspiration is available from many sources and it may well be possible to combine elements from favourite designs, or to incorporate a motif from the bridal gown or wedding stationery. An imaginative use of a seasonal theme, such as spring flowers for an Easter wedding cake, can be most attractive. The delicate beauty of tulle work, or the somewhat easier technique of rice paper, is ideal for three-dimensional centrepieces or shaped side decorations such as bells; and piping tube embroidery can be used to achieve a fragile, lacy effect, which could replicate the bride's dress or veil. Whilst over-decorating is to be avoided as it looks too fussy, bare areas need to be planned carefully and may be more appropriate for the smooth finish of a sugarpaste-covered cake. The cake design may well evolve as the work proceeds and the cake takes on its own unique character.

Tiers

If a tiered cake is to be used, it is traditional to have a 5cm (2") or 7.5cm (3") graduation between the tiers on a royal iced cake, with the top tier(s) decreasing in depth. However, sugarpaste-covered cakes may well have a 7.5cm (3") difference in diameter, with the depth of the tiers remaining the same. But, if a vase of flowers is to form the centrepiece, then a difference of only 5cm (2") forms a more pleasing overall line. Pillars for a royal iced cake should decrease in height accordingly, whilst the depth of pillars on sugarpaste-covered cakes remains the same. If a sugarpaste-covered cake is used for a tiered design, special wooden supports are available to go inside hollow pillars as sugarpaste will not support the weight of an upper tier. The preliminary section of this book includes advice on pillaring and supporting (see p.37) and also on the appropriate icing for a royal iced tiered cake (see p.18).

The cake boards used for a tiered cake should be the same size as that of the tier below, with a proportionately larger board used for the bottom tier. It is important to use boards of the same thickness for tiered cakes, and fruit cake should always be placed on a 2cm (½") drum cake board to support the weight.

The designs for tiered cakes may well need to be proportionately reduced for each tier, particularly if frills, flowers or extension work is used, as otherwise the top tier will look unwieldy or top-heavy. Separate templates will be needed for each tier and these must be carefully scaled down to ensure that they fit exactly. A quick sketch of the finished design is extremely helpful, particularly if templates, collars, runouts, etc, are to be made.

Boards

The cake board or stand is a vital part of the design process, and unusual stands can often be hired from specialist shops, or original boards cut from wood and then covered. Covering a board creates a unique look for a cake and the covering may be fabric or wrapping paper. Many of the foil papers now available are ideal for producing a subtle sheen. Paper covering should be stuck to the board with laundry starch or cornflour, whilst fabric can be stuck with a special fabric adhesive (care must be taken not to mark the fabric) or gathered with running stitches and pulled up to enclose the whole board. The covering should always extend to the back of the board, and boards for tiered cakes will need an extra circle stuck to the back. Ribbon can then be used to cover the edge of the board. This should be pinned, rather than glued into place as glue may stain the ribbon. Boards may also be covered with two coats of royal icing around the ready-positioned cake, or the cake and board can be covered in sugarpaste (see p.22).

Timing

The cake(s) should be made at least eight weeks prior to the wedding and care should be taken not to add too much alcohol during this period as it may work through the marzipan and eventually discolour the icing. The marzipan coating should be completed four weeks prior to the required date (see p.22) and the royal icing or sugarpaste one week beforehand. Allow the royal icing or sugarpaste to dry for twenty-four hours before commencing the decoration. If sugar flowers or other sugarcraft decorations are to be used, these can be made prior to decoration and stored in cardboard boxes until required (always refer to the drying times for sugarcraft items before commencing work and allow plenty of time to practise if unfamiliar items are being prepared).

The completed wedding cake should be kept in cardboard boxes in a warm dry atmosphere and away from direct sunlight.

Assembly

The cake should be transported to the reception with each tier in a separate box on the floor or in the boot of the car (never on the seat). The cake should then be tiered and assembled in its final position.

PRISCILLA

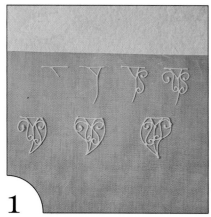

1

Using templates, pipe in royal icing (No.0) on waxed paper: 5 of A, 24 of B and C, 8 of D and E, and 5 of F and G (see p.228). Leave to dry 24 hrs.

2

Transfer template design to rectangular cake. Use H for long sides, and I for short sides. Make cuts where indicated and insert ribbons.

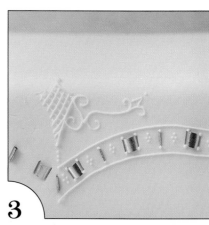

3

Pipe embroidery trellis and scrolls in royal icing (No.0). Pipe curved lines and dots around and between the ribbon inserts (No.0).

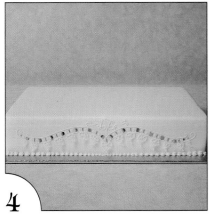

4

Remove lace and fix to long sides with small dots (No.0). Support each piece at same angle until dry. Pipe shells around cake-base (No.5).

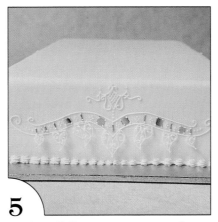

5

Fix lace (following instructions from step 4) to the shorter cake-sides.

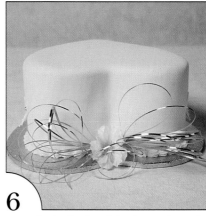

6

Neaten the back of the heart-shaped cake with a bow of ribbon loops. Add a silk flower to the centre, as shown.

7

Follow steps 2-5 to decorate the top tier, using template H and piping the embroidery trellis at the point of the heart, as shown (No.1).

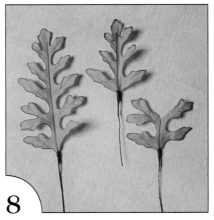

8

Wire silk leaves (see p.241) cutting each to the required size, if necessary.

9

Wire a selection of silk blossoms and ribbon loops (see p.241) and tape up the first spray.

10

Make ribbon loops using a ribbon shredder for multi-strand loops. Complete the spray as shown. Make a second spray for the bottom tier.

11

Make a shorter spray, higher at the back, for the top tier. Neaten the back of the spray with a flower and ribbon bow.

12

Position separator in centre of bottom tier. Fix sprays with royal icing or moistened sugarpaste. Fix spray to top tier before placing on separator.

TEMPLATES

G

F

E

D

C

B

A

I

H

RACHEL

1 Mould a cone of marzipan, as shown. Leave to dry for 24 hours. 32 cones required for each tier.

2 Using stiffened royal icing with no glycerin, pipe the centre of a rose on each cone (No.57) in various shades of one colour.

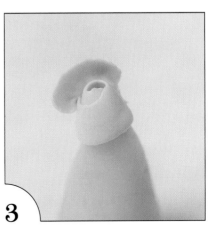

3 Pipe a petal behind the centre of each rose.

4

Pipe the next two petals, starting inside the previously piped petal.

5

Continue piping petals around the outside of the rose.

6

Continue piping further petals (at a flatter angle) to fan out the rose. Leave to dry for 24 hours then remove from the cone.

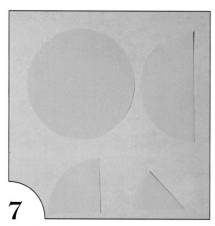

7

Cut out a paper circle and fold in half. Fold twice more in half and then cut the outer edge into a deep curve.

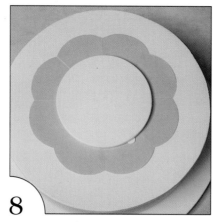

8

Unfold the template and place it onto the cake-top. Use a flat weight to hold the paper down.

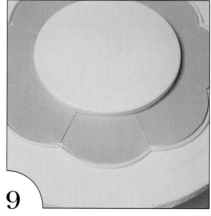

9

Pipe a line of royal icing around the edge of the template to form scallops (No.3). Remove template.

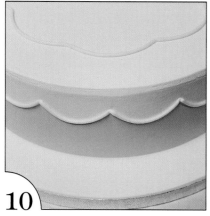

10

Fold paper band (circumference of cake) into 16. Cut a deep curve, unfold and hold against cake-side. Pipe line around cake-side (No.3).

11

Carefully remove the paper templates and then pipe a scalloped line around the cake board (No.3).

12

Pipe a line beside each No.3 line (No.2).

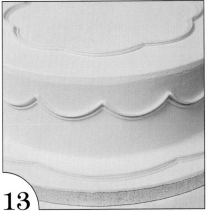

13
Overpipe each No.3 line (No.2).

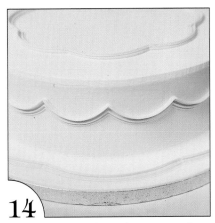

14
Pipe a line beside each outer No.2 line (No.1).

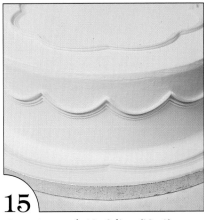

15
Overpipe each No.2 line (No.1).

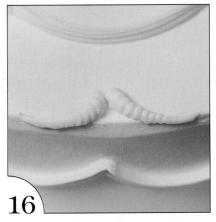

16
Pipe pairs of 'C' scrolls around the edge of the cake-top (No.3).

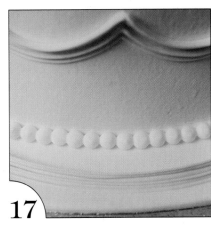

17
Pipe bulbs around the cake-base (No.2).

18
Overpipe each of the 'C' scrolls (No.2).

19
Fix roses between the 'C' scrolls and pipe a series of dots at each side (No.1).

20
Fix a rose at intervals around cake-base. Pipe dots on the board under each base rose (No.1). Pipe dots between each scallop on cake board.

21
Fix 3 roses in the centre of each cake-top below the top tier and pipe a series of dots in between (No.1) as shown.

BELINDA

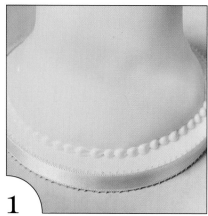

1 Cover a bell-shaped cake in sugarpaste. Fix ribbon around the cake board. Pipe shells of royal icing around cake-base (No.2).

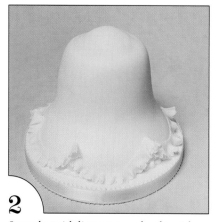

2 Scratch guidelines around cake-side. Make a Garrett frill from 455g (1lb) of sugarpaste mixed with 1 teaspoon of gum tragacanth. Fix to the cake.

3 Make and fix a second frill to the cake, approximately 6mm (¼") above the first frill.

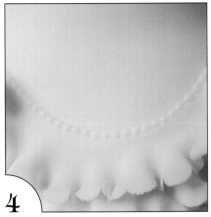

4 Pipe shells along the top edge of the frills (No.1).

Using the template as a guide, transfer the embroidery design to the cake-side then pipe (No.1).

6 Using the template as a guide, transfer the design to the cake-top and pipe embroidery pattern (No.1).

7 Pipe shells around the cake board edge (No.2) as shown.

8 Fix a small ball of sugarpaste to the cake-top and insert ribbon loops, as shown.

9 Insert flowers into the sugarpaste ball, taking care that wires do not penetrate the surface of the cake.

TEMPLATES

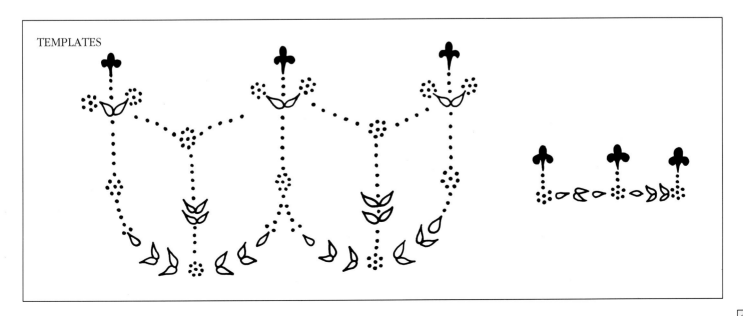

BERNICE

1

Cut various-sized blossoms from Mexican paste and frill edges with a cocktail stick. Leave to dry in a cornflour-dusted tray for 24 hours.

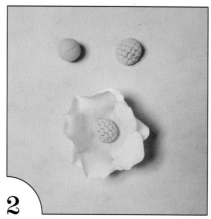

2

When dry, brush centres and edges with dusting powder. Push small balls of paste into netting to form stamens and fix into blossom centres.

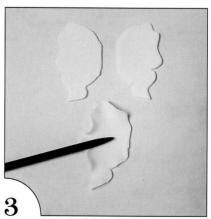

3

Cut 2 pairs of butterfly wings from Mexican paste. Frill the edges with a cocktail stick and leave to dry for 24 hours.

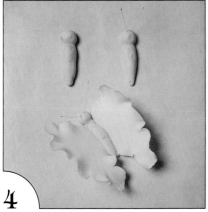

4

Dust edges of wings. Using royal icing, pipe head and body onto waxed paper (No.2). Insert wings and stamens. Support for 24 hours.

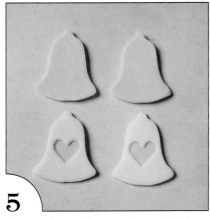

5

Cut out hearts from a sheet of white sugarpaste. Fix sheet to coloured paste and cut bell shapes (approximately 70 required per tier).

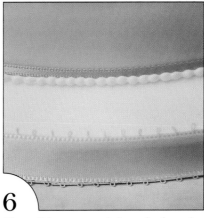

6

Fix a ribbon around the cake board edge and a narrow ribbon around the cake-base. Pipe shells of royal icing around the cake-base (No.1).

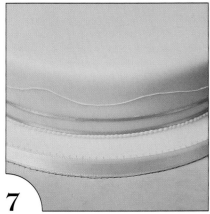

7

Fix a second narrow ribbon to cake-side. Pipe a wavy line around the cake-side (No.1).

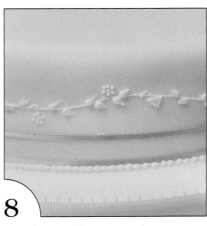

8

Pipe leaves, blossoms and grapes along the wavy line (No.1).

9

To give the blossoms height, fix a wedge of sugarpaste to the cake-top using royal icing. Begin to fix the blossoms on the wedge, as shown.

10

Fix the remaining blossoms to the cake-top using royal icing, arranging the blossoms in a crescent shape, as shown.

11

Fix the bells to cake-side with royal icing. Fix the butterfly to the cake-top to complete the bottom tier.

12

Picture shows the completed top tier cake.

PAMELA

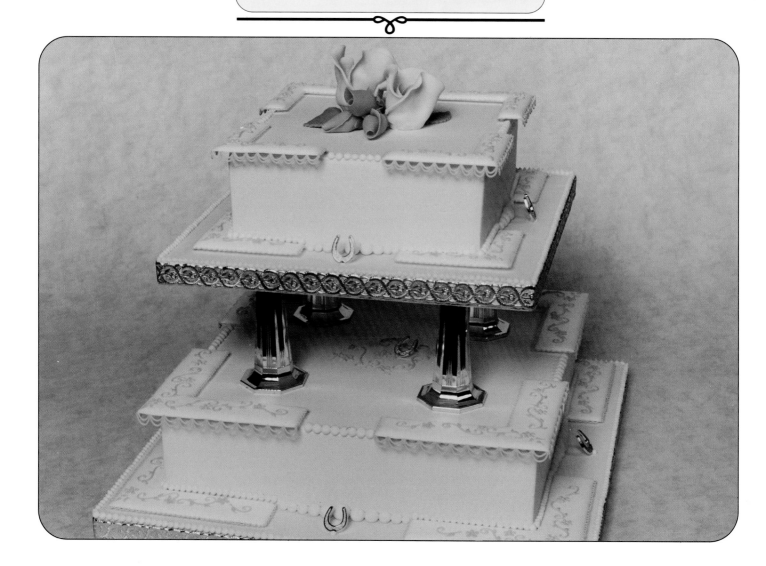

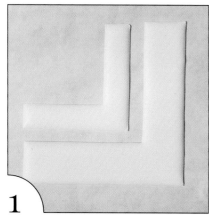

1

Using templates as guides, outline and flood-in corners onto waxed paper (No.1). Leave to dry 24 hours. 8 corners required per tier.

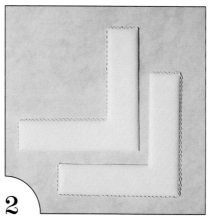

2

Pipe scallops along the inside edges of the top corner runouts and along the outside edges of the base corner runouts (No.0).

3

Pipe scrolls of varying shape and size onto each corner runout (No.1).

4

Pipe leaf and flower motifs in royal icing around the piped scrolls, as shown (No.1).

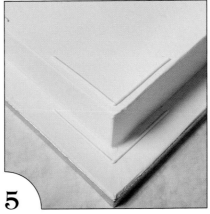

5

Pipe a line around each cake corner (No.3) and leave to dry for 30 minutes.

6

Remove the corner pieces from the waxed paper. Overpipe the board No.3 lines (No.2) and fix corner runouts to the base, as shown.

7

Pipe bulbs along the inside edge of the base runouts (No.2).

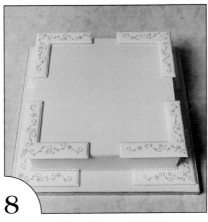

8

Overpipe the cake-top No.3 lines (No.2) and fix the top corner runouts.

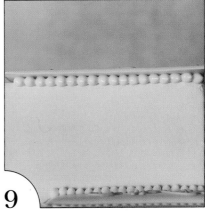

9

Pipe bulbs underneath each top corner runout (No.2).

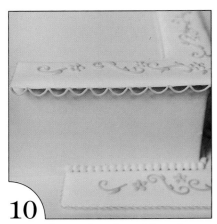

10

Pipe a dropped scalloped line along the outer edge of each cake-top corner runout (No.1).

11

Pipe a second scalloped line (No.1), as shown.

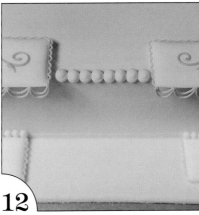

12

Pipe bulbs along the cake-top edge between each runout (No.2).

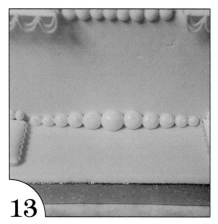

13 Starting at the centre, pipe a series of graduated bulbs between each base runout (No.3).

14 Pipe bulbs around the cake board edge (No.2).

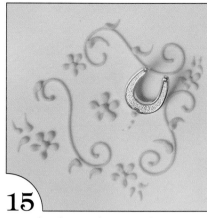

15 Pipe the design shown in the centre of the bottom tier (No.1) and fix a horseshoe to complete the decoration.

TEMPLATES

Note: Trace, cut out and place cardboard templates onto coated cake to check for correct proportions (see p.32).

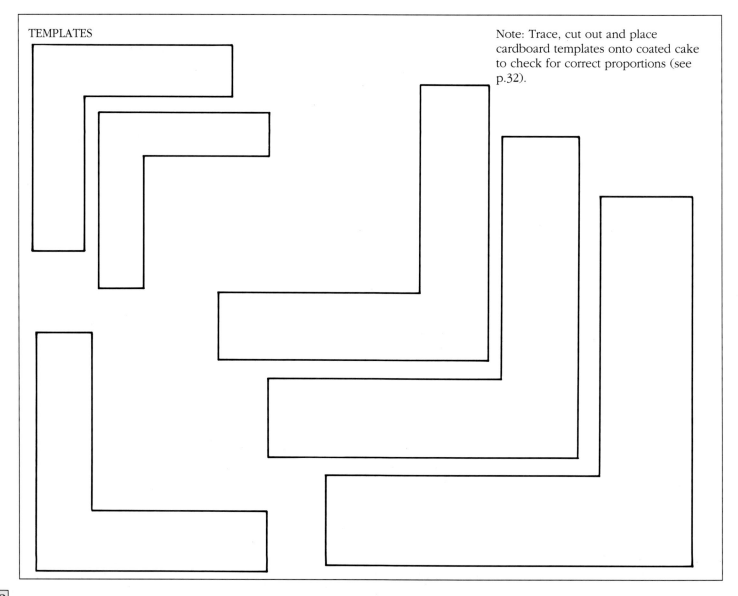

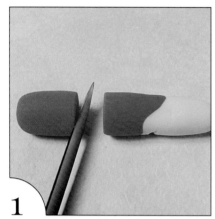

1

Colour 30g (1oz) of sugarpaste to darkest shade. Put half aside as colour sample No.1. Knead remaining with 15g (½oz) of white paste.

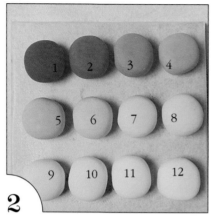

2

Continue dividing in half and adding white sugarpaste until there are 11 colour samples. Use 15g (½oz) of white sugarpaste as the 12th sample.

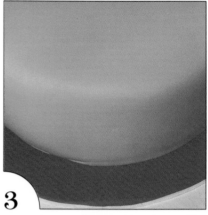

3

Cover large cake in colour 4. Mix ½ tsp. of gum tragacanth into 60g (2oz) of matching paste, reserve for frills. Cover board in shade 1.

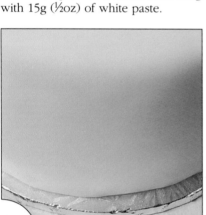

4

Cover medium cake to match colour sample 8. Add gum tragacanth to 60g (2oz) as in step 3. Cover small cake with white sugarpaste.

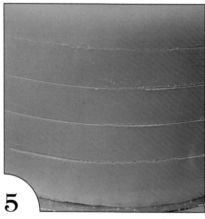

5

Place medium and small cakes on small, thin boards. Referring to the templates on p.243, score guidelines for frills onto all cakes.

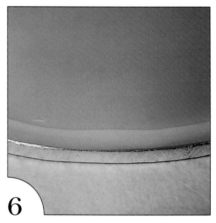

6

Fix long thin rolls of sugarpaste around the cake-bases, matching colour No.1 for bottom tier, No.5 for middle tier, and No.9 for top tier.

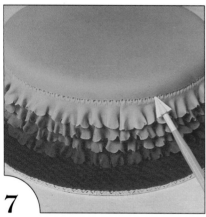

7

Make 4 frills matching colours 1-4 and fix around the sides of the large cake. Indent the edge of the top frill with a modelling tool to neaten.

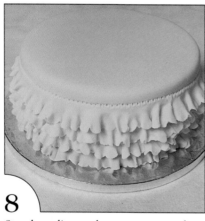

8

Stand medium cake on a spare cake board. Matching colours 5-8, make and fix 4 rows of frills (the bottom row to overlap edge of thin board).

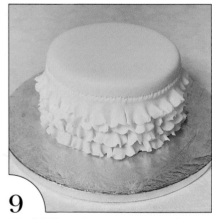

9

Fix 4 frills in the same way to the small cake, matching colours 9-12, as shown.

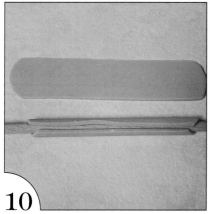

10 Cut a strip of No.4 sugarpaste mixed with the gum tragacanth and wrap around a skewer. Moisten edges to join. Smooth and neaten.

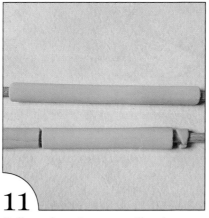

11 Roll gently to improve pillar shape. Cut pillar to 9cm (3½") long. Make another 2 pillars in spare colour No.4, and 3 in spare colour No.8.

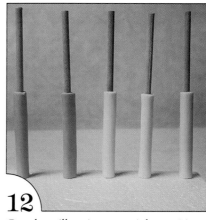

12 Dry the pillars in an upright position. Remove from the skewers when just dry enough to hold their shape. Leave to dry for 24 hours.

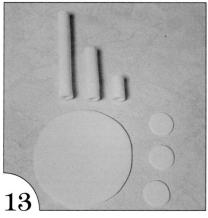

13 Make top ornament from paste mixed with gum tragacanth. Pedestals 11.5, 6.5 and 2.5cm (4½", 2½" and 1") long. Leave to dry.

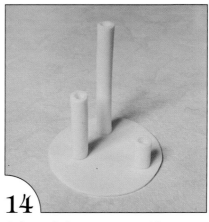

14 Soften a little sugarpaste with egg white to form a sticky paste and use to fix the pedestals to the base in the marked positions. Leave to dry.

15 Remove small silk leaves from plastic stems. Hold hooked wire behind leaf and wind long leg around short leg, trapping in leaf base. Twist and tape.

16 Lengthen large leaves with wire by threading it through material behind the central vein. Secure and neaten with tape.

17 Wind wire around flower head behind calyx. Wind long leg of wire around short leg and stem. Secure and neaten with tape.

18 Small flowers can be wired singly with a hook behind the stem, or in groups. Twist long leg around short leg. Secure and neaten with tape.

19

Start to make a spray using a large leaf, bright blossoms and ribbons, tapering the stem length.

20

Continue enlarging the spray, taping the wires to the main stem.

21

Widen the arrangement at the base of the spray, then cut wires to a taper.

22

Tape the tapered wires together, adding large blossoms, as shown. Fold under the spray. 3 sprays required.

23

Repeat steps 19-22 using paler shades of blossom, as shown.

24

Make 3 sprays of very pale blossoms and ribbons for the top ornament.

25

Position the sprays on top of the large and medium cakes, as shown.

26

Paint pillars with confectioners' glaze. Mark pillar positions and insert skewers (see p.37). Fix pillars and flower sprays.

27

Pipe shells around foot of pedestals and edge of base (No.1). Glaze. Fix ribbon spirals and flowers to pedestals. Leave to dry.

TEMPLATES

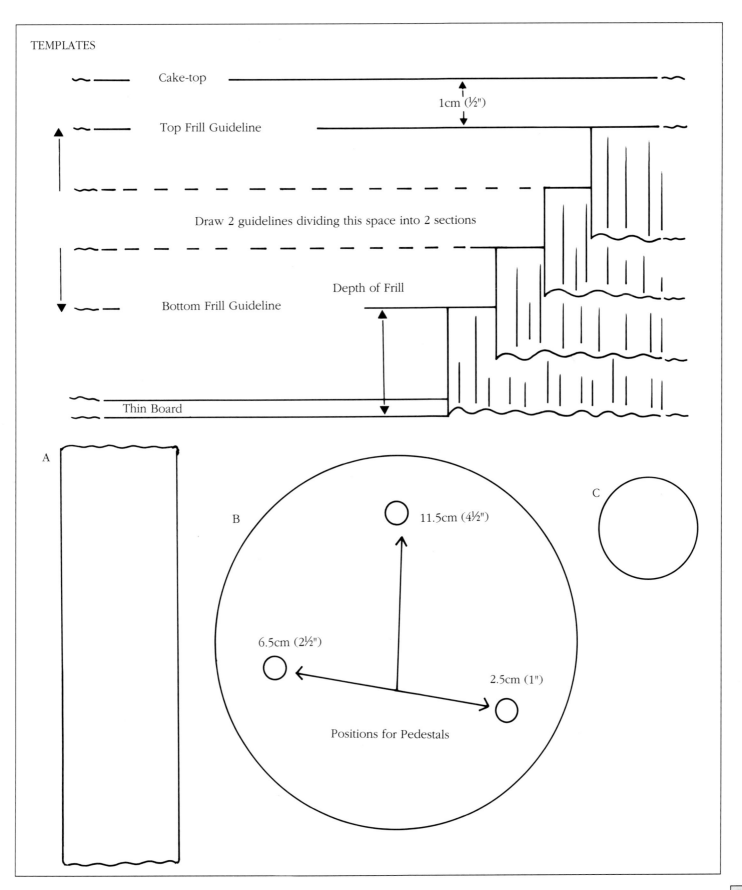

Cake-top

1cm (½")

Top Frill Guideline

Draw 2 guidelines dividing this space into 2 sections

Depth of Frill

Bottom Frill Guideline

Thin Board

A

B

C

11.5cm (4½")

6.5cm (2½")

2.5cm (1")

Positions for Pedestals

CHARLOTTE

1

Pick suitable, edible flowers, ensuring they are clean, dry and have not been sprayed with insecticide. Crystallise within 1 hour of picking.

2

Add 2 teaspoons of cold water to 1 fresh egg white in a clean, grease-free bowl and mix thoroughly.

3

Gently cover the top surface of the flower petals with egg white, using a soft, medium-sized paintbrush.

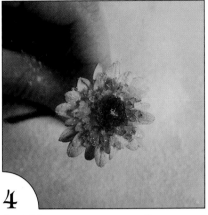

4
Sprinkle caster sugar over flower.
Shake off excess. Sugar can be
coloured with confectioners' dusting
powder or edible food colouring.

5
Repeat steps 3-4 for back of petals.
When all flowers have been treated in
this way, place on greaseproof paper
and leave to dry for 24 hours.

6
Repeat steps 1-5 for Maidenhair fern.

7
Make ribbon loops and fix, with the
flowers and fern, around the cake-
base.

8
Pipe motif, as shown (No.1). Pipe 'S'
and 'C' scrolls either side of motif
(No.2).

9
Fix sugar dove (see p.246) and link
scrolls with scalloped lines (No.1).

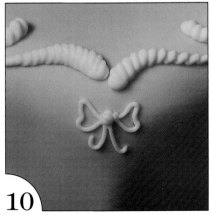

10
Pipe a bow at each cake-top corner
(No.1).

11
Fix flowers, fern and loops in the
centre of the bottom tier, as shown.

12
Mount and fix flowers, fern and
ribbon onto a dome of sugarpaste to
form a posy for the top tier.

LEANNE

1
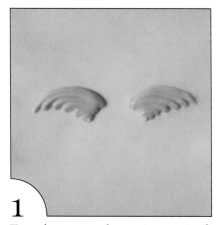

To make a sugar dove, pipe a pair of wings onto waxed paper (No.1). Leave to dry for 24 hours.

2

Pipe the dove's tail, body, head and beak onto waxed paper (No.1).

3

Whilst still wet, fix the wings to the body and leave to dry for 24 hours.

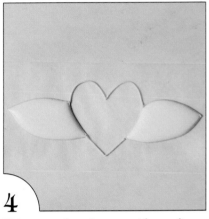

4 Using template A as a guide, outline and flood-in the parts shown with soft royal icing (No.1). Leave to dry for 2 hours. 4 required per tier.

5 Flood-in the heart centre and leave to dry for 24 hours.

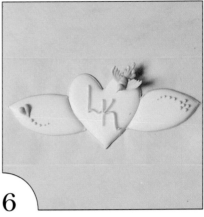

6 Decorate the runouts (No.1). Fix the sugar doves.

7 Remove the dry runouts from the waxed paper and fix to the cake-top.

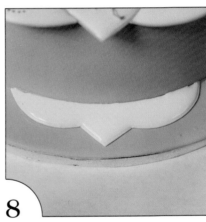

8 Following the shape of the top design, outline and flood-in the base design (No.2).

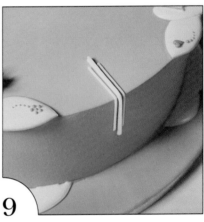

9 Pipe a series of graduated lines over the cake-top edge (No's.3 and 2).

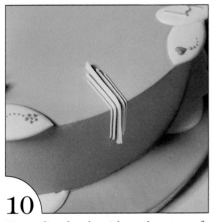

10 Pipe a line by the side and on top of each No.2 line (No.1).

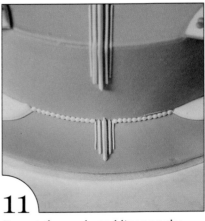

11 Repeat the graduated lines on the cake board. Pipe shells either side, as shown (No.2).

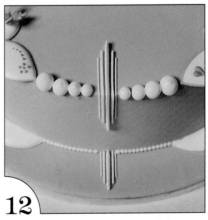

12 Pipe graduated bulbs around the cake-top edge (No.3).

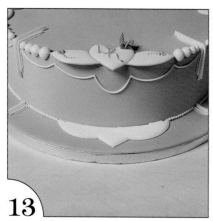

13
Pipe a series of scalloped lines on the cake-side (No.2).

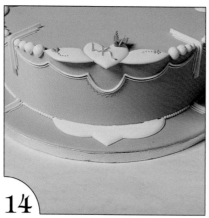

14
Pipe a line by the side and on top of the No.2 line (No.1). Pipe a scalloped border, as shown (No.1).

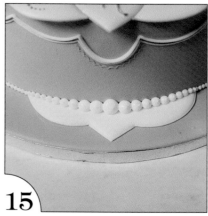

15
Pipe graduated bulbs around the cake-base (No.3).

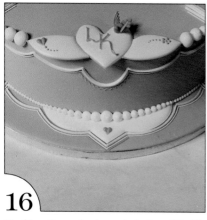

16
Outline the cake board design (No.2). Pipe a line by the side and on top of the No.2 line (No.1). Complete with a heart motif and scalloped line.

17
Fix a decorative heart to the centre of the cake-top. Pipe initials of choice, as shown (No.1).

18
Decorate the heart with motifs and love birds. Repeat steps 1-16 for top tier, using template B.

TEMPLATES

A

B

1

Using template A, cut 65 bridge sections from flower paste. Place in former, ensuring each piece is lying straight across. Leave to dry.

2

Dust inside the bell mould with cornflour and support the mould, as shown. Cut off the point of a wooden skewer and smooth the end.

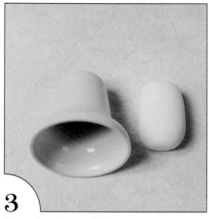

3

Knead a piece of flower paste, approximately the size of the body of the bell. Form the paste into a roll, as shown.

4

Insert prepared skewer into centre of paste roll, pushing it nearly to the end but not through. Roll on skewer to smooth outside and widen hole.

5

Push the opened paste roll into the bell mould, rotating it with a finger to smooth the surface and applying pressure to thin the paste.

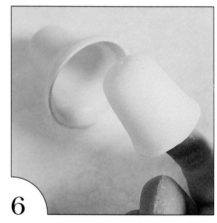

6

Repeatedly tip the developing bell shape out of the mould to prevent sticking. Dust with more cornflour if necessary.

7

Using a finger or thumb, smooth and thin the paste towards edge of mould. Trim off surplus paste. Remove and replace to prevent sticking.

8

Open out a scalloped crimper. Using one edge only, push through the paste to make scallops around the edge of the bell. Remove surplus.

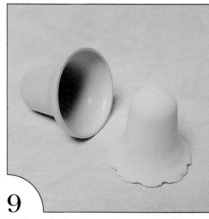

9

Make a hole in top for cord. When set enough to hold its shape, remove bell. Leave to dry 24 hours. 11 large and 5 small bells required.

10

Form a ball of paste, about the size of a large pea. Thread onto hooked rose wire, burying hook. Leave to dry in cornflour. 16 required.

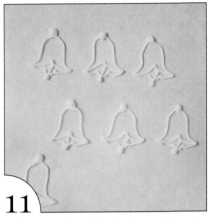

11

Using template B, pipe lace pieces in royal icing onto waxed paper or easy-off plastic (No.1 or 0). 140 required.

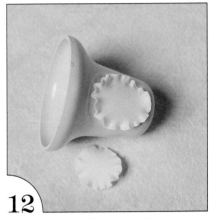

12

Roll out modelling paste. Using templates C and D for the plaques, cut 2 of each shape. Frill edges and leave to dry over a bell mould.

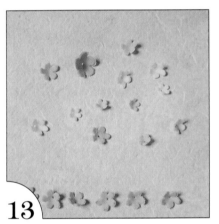

13

Make a selection of sugarpaste blossoms for decorating the bells and borders.

14

Make 4 full roses, 3 half roses and 3 buds, 4 carnations and a selection of small filler flowers from flower paste. Leave to dry.

15

Make 4 double ribbon tails and approximately 30 finger loops. Make 16 leaves of various sizes from flower paste. Leave to dry.

16

Using a strip of soft tissue and sticky tape, make a 'hat' to protect bells while holding for dusting. Dust edges of bells and small plaques.

17

Put 2 large and 1 small bell to one side. Decorate the remainder of the bells, as shown.

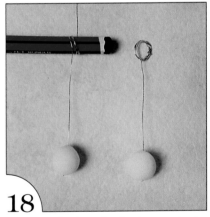

18

Measure the length of wire required for each clapper. Wind the remainder of the wire around a pencil and secure to make a firm ring, as shown.

19

With the aid of a thin, bent wire, thread the cords through each bell and tie to the wire rings. Fix clappers into each bell.

20

Tape up a slender spray of prepared flowers and ribbon loops to fit into one of the selected large bells put to one side.

21

Pipe royal icing inside top of bell. Fill half the bell with sugarpaste. Press stem of spray into the paste, filling gaps with ribbon loops.

22

Fill the second reserved large bell with a shorter spray. Tape up and fix a spray into the small bell. Decorate back of each bell with piping (No.0).

23

Using a suitable stand, hang a bell from the hook. Conceal knot with small ribbon bow. Fix a full rose, few fillers and ribbon loops to base.

24

Mark line for top of extension. Using 6mm (¼") strip of paper as a guide, push sections into cake-side. Pipe shells around cake-base (No.1).

25

Fix ribbons from extension guideline to below bridge joins. Fix blossoms and pipe leaves, as shown.

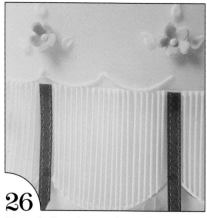

26

Pipe shallow loops above the extensions (No.1). Pipe extension lines (No.0). (The ribbons will help to keep the piping straight).

27

Fix the lace pieces with a dot of royal icing to the top of each loop. Neaten the bottom of the extension with piped loops (No.0).

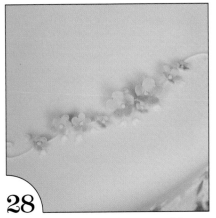

28
Pipe stems with royal icing and fix a small arrangement of blossoms on both tiers (No.0).

29
For the top tier, cut a thin cake card 6mm (¼") smaller than the cake board and firmly wire it to top of stand. Position cakes, as shown.

30
Position and fix 2 large filled bells to bottom tier. Fix the medium filled bell to the middle tier.

31
Attach some hanging bells by making holes through cake card and secure with sticky tape. Attach others taking cord over card edge and securing.

32
When in final position, bring cords from filled bells up over card edge and secure. Place small tier on top of card and add top decoration.

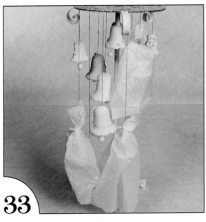

33
If cake is to be transported, wrap tissue around each bell and fix with wire twist before securing stand upright in box. Pack more tissue.

TEMPLATES

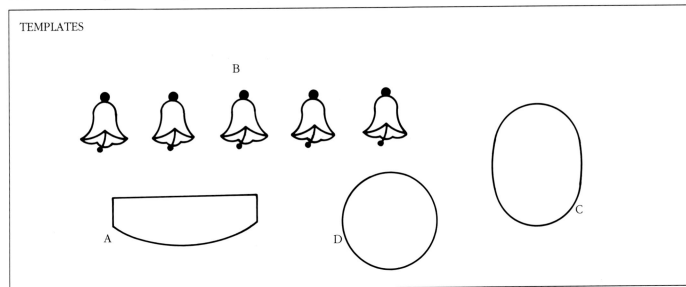

101 Cake Designs

ISBN: 0 946429 00 6   320 pages
The original Mary Ford definite cake artistry text book. A classic in its field, over 250,000 copies sold.

Another 101 Cake Designs

ISBN: 0 946429 01 4   320 pages
A further 101 deliciously different and original Mary Ford cake designs with full instructions for each stage.

The Concise Book of Cake Making and Decorating

ISBN: 0 946429 07 3   96 pages
Mary Ford divulges all the skills and techniques cake decorators need to make and decorate a variety of cakes in every medium.

Making Cakes for Money

ISBN: 0 946429 11 1   120 pages
A practical workbook for accurately costing each stage of cake production and determining how much to charge customers.

Chocolate Cookbook

ISBN: 0 946429 18 9   96 pages
A complete introduction to cooking with chocolate featuring sweets, luscious gateaux, rich desserts and Easter Eggs.

Jams, Chutneys and Pickles

IBSN: 0 946429 33 2   96 pages
Over 70 of Mary Ford's favourite recipes for delicious jams, jellies, pickles and chutneys with hints and tips for perfect results.

Sugarpaste Cake Decorating

ISBN: 0 946429 10 3   96 pages
27 innovative Mary Ford cake designs illustrating royal icing decoration on sugarpaste covered cakes.

Children's Cakes

ISBN: 0 946429 35 9   96 pages
32 exciting new Mary Ford designs and templates for children's cakes in a wide range of mediums.

Party Cakes

ISBN: 0 946429 09 X   120 pages
36 superb party time sponge cake designs and templates for tots to teenagers. An invaluable prop for the party cake decorator.

Sugar Flowers Cake Decorating

ISBN: 0 946429 12 X   96 pages
Practical, easy-to-follow pictorial instructions for making and using superb, natural looking sugar flowers for cakes.

A Cake For All Seasons

ISBN: 0 946429 08 1   120 pages
A different cake recipe for every month of the year with a host of new cake designs and seasonal decorations.

Decorative Sugar Flowers for Cakes

ISBN: 0 946429 28 6   120 pages
33 of the highest quality handcrafted sugar flowers with cutter shapes, background information and appropriate uses.

Sugarcraft Cake Decorating

ISBN: 0 946429 30 8   96 pages
A definitive sugarcraft book featuring an extensive selection of exquisite sugarcraft items designed and made by Pat Ashby.

Writing in Icing

ISBN: 0 946429 02 2   96 pages
How to make cakes talk. An invaluable guide to achieving a professional standard when piping decorative lettering on cakes.

Making Soft Toys

ISBN: 0 946429 20 0   120 pages
A structured, step-by-step course with 21 appealing soft toys, with templates, designed and graded for easy making.

Making Teddy Bears

ISBN: 946429 32 4   96 pages
11 new Teddy Bear designs, with templates, ranging from traditional to jointed, modern and novelty Teddy items.

Making Glove Puppets

ISBN: 0 946429 26 X   96 pages
14 specially designed fun glove puppets with full size templates and step-by-step instructions for each stage.